2 CORINTHIANS

J. Vernon McGee

THOMAS NELSON PUBLISHERS

Nashville • Atlanta • London • Vancouver

Published in Nashville, Tennessee, by Thomas Nelson, Inc.

Scripture quotations are from the KING JAMES VERSION of the Bible.

Library of Congress Cataloging-in-Publication Data

McGee, J. Vernon (John Vernon), 1904–1988
    [Thru the Bible with J. Vernon McGee]
    Thru the Bible commentary series / J. Vernon McGee.
      p.   cm.
    Reprint. Originally published: Thru the Bible with J. Vernon McGee. 1975.
    Includes bibliographical references.
    ISBN 0-7852-1049-0 (TR)
    ISBN 0-7852-1109-8 (NRM)
    1. Bible—Commentaries. I. Title.
BS491.2.M37 1991
220.7'7—dc20   90–41340
                                      CIP

Printed in the United States of America

24 25 26 27 28 29 30 — 04 03 02 01

CONTENTS

2 CORINTHIANS

PREFACE

The radio broadcasts of the Thru the Bible Radio five-year program were transcribed, edited, and published first in single-volume paperbacks to accommodate the radio audience.

There has been a minimal amount of further editing for this publication. Therefore, these messages are not the word-for-word recording of the taped messages which went out over the air. The changes were necessary to accommodate a reading audience rather than a listening audience.

These are popular messages, prepared originally for a radio audience. They should not be considered a commentary on the entire Bible in any sense of that term. These messages are devoid of any attempt to present a theological or technical commentary on the Bible. Behind these messages is a great deal of research and study in order to interpret the Bible from a popular rather than from a scholarly (and too-often boring) viewpoint.

We have definitely and deliberately attempted "to put the cookies on the bottom shelf so that the kiddies could get them."

The fact that these messages have been translated into many languages for radio broadcasting and have been received with enthusiasm reveals the need for a simple teaching of the whole Bible for the masses of the world.

I am indebted to many people and to many sources for bringing this volume into existence. I should express my especial thanks to my secretary, Gertrude Cutler, who supervised the editorial work; to Dr. Elliott R. Cole, my associate, who handled all the detailed work with the publishers; and finally, to my wife Ruth for tenaciously encouraging me from the beginning to put my notes and messages into printed form.

Solomon wrote, ". . . of making many books there is no end; and much study is a weariness of the flesh" (Eccl. 12:12). On a sea of books that flood the marketplace, we launch this series of THRU THE BIBLE with the hope that it might draw many to the one Book, The Bible.

J. VERNON McGEE

The Second Epistle to the
CORINTHIANS

INTRODUCTION

The author of the epistle is Paul. Paul had written First Corinthians from Ephesus where he had been engaged in a great ministry. He had written, "For a great door and effectual is opened unto me, and there are many adversaries" (1 Cor. 16:9). I believe that Paul had his greatest ministry in Asia Minor—Ephesus being the springboard and the sounding board for the gospel. I believe that the gospel covered that area in a manner that was probably more effective than it has ever been in any other place at any other time. That is what Paul meant—"For a great door and effectual is opened unto me."

Because of that ministry, Paul just couldn't leave and go over to Corinth. In Corinth was that baby church which he had started. That church was filled with carnal Christians. They acted like babies. They wanted Paul to come, because they wanted attention. They wanted food and they wanted a change of garments—I guess you could say they were all wet. They were crying as babies cry. Paul couldn't come, and they were a little miffed and a little hurt by it. So Paul had written his first letter and had told them that he would be coming later.

Paul remained in Ephesus approximately three years. He didn't get to Corinth, and the Corinthians were still disturbed. He had sent Titus to Corinth because he could not personally go there at that time. Timothy had been with Paul in Ephesus, and these two left Ephesus and proceeded to Troas to wait for Titus to bring word from Corinth (see 2 Cor. 2:12–13). When Titus did not come, Paul and Timothy went on to Philippi. It was there that Titus met them and brought Paul word about the Corinthians. He brought good news from Corinth—that the Corinthians were obeying the things that Paul had told them to do in his first answer to their questions; that is, in First Corinthians.

At Philippi Paul sat down to write this second epistle. The Corinthians still wanted the great apostle to come and be with them. However, any breach between Paul and the Corinthian church was healed. In this epistle Paul opens his heart in a very wonderful way. To tell the truth, Paul lets us come to know him better personally in this epistle than in any other letter.

Second Corinthians deals with conditions of the *ministry* within the church. (First Corinthians dealt with conditions and *corrections* in the church.)

OUTLINE

This epistle is difficult to outline, as it is less organized than any of Paul's other letters, but it contains more personal details. In each chapter there is always a minor theme developed, which sometimes seems to take the place of the major theme and is generally expressed in some striking verse. This may explain the seeming difficulty in outlining and organizing this epistle. We will note this as we consider each chapter.

CHAPTER 1

THEME: God's comfort for life's plans

The first two verses are an introduction to the epistle. Then the rest of chapter 1 is about God's comfort for life's plans. Paul really begins this epistle on a high note.

INTRODUCTION

Paul, an apostle of Jesus Christ by the will of God, and Timothy our brother, unto the church of God which is at Corinth, with all the saints which are in all Achaia [2 Cor. 1:1].

Paul is writing in the *authority* of "an apostle." I feel that any minister today should speak with authority. There is no use trying to give out God's Word unless the speaker is convinced of the truth of it himself. If he isn't speaking the Word with authority, then he ought to start selling insurance, or work in a filling station, or do something else. He should not be in the ministry. We already have too many men who are unsure that the Bible actually is the Word of God—that is the weakness of the contemporary church.

In the early church, when persecution began, the believers said, "O Lord, Thou art God." My friend, if you are not sure that He is God, you are not sure of anything. And they were sure of the Word of God. They rested upon it at all times. And Paul writes with this authority.

Paul was an apostle "by the will of God." You can't go any higher than that. That is authority. If your life is in the will of God, there is no question in your mind. If you are in the will of God, it makes no difference *where* you are or *how* you are or *what* your circumstances may be, you are in a wonderful, glorious place. You may even be lying in a hospital bed. If that is the will of God, that is the proper place for you. I have a friend who is a music director, and he generally begins a song service on some humorous note. I heard him say one time, "Wouldn't you rather be here than in the best hospital in town?" I have always laughed about that, but I have also thought about it a great deal. If it is God's will for you to be in the best hospital in town, then that is the greatest place for you to be.

"And Timothy our brother." I love that. He is a Christian brother to Paul and to the church at Corinth. In another place Paul calls Timothy his son in the faith. However, when Paul is writing to the church, he puts Timothy right on a par with himself. I love the way Paul has of putting others on the same plane with himself.

"Unto the church of God"—this is God's church we are talking about. I hear people say, "My church," and sometimes they act as if it were their church. They forget that it is God's church, that it is the church of the Lord Jesus Christ which He purchased with His blood. In view of the fact that He paid such a price for the church, you and I better not be cheap Christians, expressing our little will in the church. Let's remember it is His church.

"Which is at Corinth, with all the saints which are in all Achaia." Paul didn't confine this to Corinth alone. Paul extended it to all Achaia because, everywhere the gospel went in that day, these people were witnesses. They carried the gospel out to others.

I have gone through that land of Achaia. It is beautiful country. They have the most beautiful grape vineyards I have ever seen anywhere. And beautiful flowers! I can visualize those early Christians, steeped in sin in the city of Corinth. Then when Paul came with the gospel, the scales fell from their eyes. The light broke upon their darkened souls. They turned from their sins to the living Christ. Then they went all over Achaia witnessing for Christ. Many were won for Christ. Paul was also talking to all of them—to "all the saints which are in all Achaia." How wonderful that is.

Now friend, the church of God which Paul happens to be addressing is this church in Corinth. The church in your hometown, the church in your neighborhood, is also God's church. Don't forget that.

Grace be to you and peace from God our Father, and from the Lord Jesus Christ [2 Cor. 1:2].

Paul uses this salutation frequently. Grace and peace are those great gifts from God to the believer.

GOD'S COMFORT IN LIFE'S PLANS

Blessed be God, even the Father of our Lord Jesus Christ, the Father of mercies, and the God of all comfort [2 Cor. 1:3].

The word for "blessed" is actually *praise*—Praise be to God. I wonder how much we really praise Him. I find that I am doing a better job of praising Him since I have retired than I did when I was a pastor.

David put it like this: "I will bless the LORD at all times: his praise shall continually be in my mouth" (Ps. 34:1). That ought to get rid of the complaining of the saints. We are to *praise* the Lord. "Whoso offereth praise glorifieth me . . ." (Ps. 50:23).

"Blessed be God, even the Father of our Lord Jesus Christ." God is the Father. That is His position in the Trinity. God so loved the world that He gave His only begotten Son. Jesus Christ wasn't begotten in the sense of being born. He is the only begotten One in the sense that He occupies a position that is totally unique. He is the eternal Son, and God is the everlasting Father. If you have a Father and a Son like that, then there never was a time when there was any begetting in the sense of being born, of having a beginning. Rather, it expresses the positions in the Trinity. They are both eternal.

Now Paul calls Him "the Father of mercies, and the God of all comfort." I want to stop here and spend a little time on three words: *love, mercy, grace.*

So much is being said today about love. It is sloppy theology to say that God saves us by His love. Now it is true that God loves us. Oh, how He loves us! We just don't know how much He loves us. It would break our hearts if we could comprehend how much God loves us. But God does not save us by His love. The Scriptures teach that we are saved by God's *grace.*

Now what is grace? We call it unmerited favor, which means that God saves us on a different basis than merit. God loves us, but He does not save us by His love. He saves us by His grace. Why? Because He is also the God of all mercies—the Father of mercies. Mercy means that God so loved us that He provided a Savior for us because He couldn't save us any other way. Anything that we have today is a mercy from God. He is the Father of mercy. In fact, He is said to be rich in grace and rich in mercy.

Do you need any mercy today? If you need money, you go to a bank to get it. If you need mercy, go to the One who is the Father of mercies. If you need any help, go to Him. After all, anything and everything that you have today is a mercy from God. You don't deserve it. I don't deserve anything that I have. I don't have much, but what I have is a mercy of God.

God was merciful to put me into the ministry. You don't know me like I know myself. If you knew me as I know myself, you wouldn't listen to me. Wait a minute—don't cut me off. If I knew you like you know yourself, I wouldn't be talking to you. I would quit right now. You see, you and I have been extended mercy, and I am in the ministry because of the mercy of God.

Now I must say something that is difficult for me to say: I have had cancer, probably still have it in my body, by the mercy of God. I hate to say it, but it is true. Everything that we have is a mercy. Not only is He the Father of mercies, He is also the God of all comfort. You can test that in the crucible of life. Suffering is the acid test. He is the God of all comfort. He will comfort you in the hospital. He will comfort you at the funeral home when you have a loved one there. He can comfort you in any place at any time. He is the God of all comfort.

There is an authentic comfort, and there is a counterfeit one. I don't like to hear people sigh and say, "God has permitted this to come to me and I accept it," when they don't accept it but rebel against it. Be honest with God. Tell Him how you feel. Tell Him you don't like what is happening to you. He knows all about it anyway. He wants you to talk frankly with Him. Comfort can be genuine or fake.

There is a popular notion that comfort is some sort of saccharine sweet sentimentality with a note of weakness. I can remember that when I was a little fellow I was always falling down and skinning my knees. I always wondered why my mother didn't put me in long pants, but she never did. When I'd skin my knee, she would kiss it and say, "It's all well now." She kidded me into thinking it was well and I would quit crying. Now that is sentiment; it's sweet and lovely. But there came a day when I went away to school and I got discouraged because I didn't have any money. Then she sat down and talked to me. It was pretty strong medicine. She said, "Now you must be a man, my son." That was comfort also.

People turn to all sorts of things for comfort. There is a whiskey called "Southern Comfort." Well, I'm a Southerner, but that is not a comfort, my friend. That will ruin a home. Others turn to drugs for comfort, but there is no comfort there.

The Greek word for "comfort" is *parakaleo*, which means "to call alongside of." The Holy Spirit is called the Paraclete. He is called to our side. When the Lord Jesus promised to send the Holy Spirit, He said, "I will not leave you comfortless . . ." (John 14:18). The word He used there is *orphanos*—"I will not leave you orphans. I will send the Comforter to you, the Paraclete." He said to His own men, ". . . It is expedient for you that I go away: for if I go not away, the Comforter will not come unto you; but if I depart, I will send him unto you" (John 16:7).

What is the Comforter then? He is not someone who simply kisses a bruise. He is a helper, a strengthener, an advocate. He is One who is called to help me and to strengthen me, to relieve the loneliness and assuage the grief and calm the fears. He means help in time of terrifying trouble. "Hear, O LORD, and have mercy upon me: LORD, be thou my helper" (Ps. 30:10). That is the cry of the soul that needs the Comforter. God is the God of all comfort.

> **Who comforteth us in all our tribulation, that we may be able to comfort them which are in any trouble, by the comfort wherewith we ourselves are comforted of God [2 Cor. 1:4].**

It is a very wonderful thing that we have a God who can comfort us in all our troubles. It is one thing to have comfort when the sun is shining and with someone patting us on the back. But, my friend, what we really need is comfort in the time of trouble.

We will see that Paul experienced that kind of comfort in his time of trouble. You see, we need the assurance of the presence of God in all the circumstances of life—in the area of our greatest need, in our loneliness, in the desperate hour of life.

Christianity is just a theory to many people. It is merely a profession; it is like a garment to be put on for special occasions and then worn lightly. It is a stagnant ritual and an empty vocabulary. My friend, may I say to you that the proof of Christianity is how it walks in shoe leather. It wasn't just a theory to the apostle Paul.

> **For as the sufferings of Christ abound in us, so our consolation also aboundeth by Christ.**

> **And whether we be afflicted, it is for your consolation and salvation, which is effectual in the enduring of the same sufferings which we also suffer: or whether we be comforted, it is for your consolation and salvation [2 Cor. 1:5–6].**

We will find that Paul is going to talk a great deal about the trouble he had and was presently having and of God's comfort through it all.

> **And our hope of you is stedfast, knowing, that as ye are partakers of the sufferings, so shall ye be also of the consolation.**

> **For we would not, brethren, have you ignorant of our trouble which came to us in Asia, that we were pressed out of measure, above strength, insomuch that we despaired even of life:**

> **But we had the sentence of death in ourselves, that we should not trust in ourselves, but in God which raiseth the dead:**

> **Who delivered us from so great a death, and doth deliver: in whom we trust that he will yet deliver us [2 Cor. 1:7–10].**

This is wonderful. This explains why God permits us to have trouble or to be sick. Paul here says that he was sick nigh unto death. In fact, he had "the sentence of death" in him. He was so ill that I think the doctor told him he would die. There are others who think he is referring to the time the mob tried to attack him in Ephesus. They would have torn Paul to pieces, and he would have been made a martyr. He could have been referring to either experience; both would have carried the sentence of death. But Paul says that God who raises the dead "delivered us from so great a death, and doth deliver: in whom we trust that he will yet deliver us." That is quite wonderful, and it ought to be practical for us today.

Let me say that God permits Christians to suffer. He has a good reason, a very wonderful purpose in it all. He intends for it to work out for the good of these believers. He intended for it to serve a good purpose so they can comfort someone else.

Everything that you and I have we have because of the mercy of God. And we have it for the benefit of others. Regardless of what you have, God has given it to you so that you can share it with others. He has given it to you as a mercy. If you have health, wealth, youth, talent, or a gift, He wants you to use it to share with others. Each issues from the mercy of God. And wait a minute—suffering also. If you are suffering for Christ, He permits that to happen to you.

Dr. Harry Ironside used to tell the story of a friend of his who was in Vienna, Austria, on a sightseeing bus trip. As they were traveling, some sheep got in the way of the bus and they were held up. The man sitting next to his friend was annoyed by it all because there were only two sheep dogs that were herding those sheep. So this friend, a Christian, said to this annoyed man sitting next to him, "Do you know the names of those two sheep dogs?" And he said, "Why, no, I don't know the names. Do you know the names?" "Yes, I think I do." "What are they?" His friend said, "One of them is named 'Goodness' and the other is named 'Mercy.'" He said, "How in the world do you know that?" "Well," he said, "I'll tell you how. David said, 'Surely goodness and mercy shall follow us all the days of our lives.'"

You might not think it was goodness and mercy to have a couple of dogs yapping at you to keep you from going to the left or to the right, but it is God's mercy that keeps us in the straight and narrow way, and He uses trial and difficulty for that very purpose. He is "the Father of mercies."

Now I am going to be personal. I had several recurrences of cancer and, I'll be frank with you, my doctor didn't offer me much hope. But God has been delivering me—it is amazing. That monster can turn on me at any moment; yet I trust that God will deliver. I received a letter from a man who to me seems arrogant. He wrote, "God has told me that you are going to get well; so you don't need to worry about it any more." I wonder, since I was the fellow who had the cancer, why didn't God tell me that? Well, I'm just waiting on the Lord. I can say with Paul that I trust He will deliver me. We cannot be arrogant with God; we need to walk softly.

Paul is walking softly, but he can say with great assurance, "He *has* delivered me from death." And he can say, "Right at the present, *He is* delivering me." And then, without any boasting, he says, "We trust that *He* will yet deliver us." Paul didn't know that He would, but he believed that He would. Therefore, on the basis of that, Paul could rejoice in the fact that God was permitting him to give out the gospel in that day.

Paul appeals to these Corinthian believers for prayer.

> **Ye also helping together by prayer for us, that for the gift bestowed upon us by the means of many persons thanks may be given by many on our behalf [2 Cor. 1:11].**

God wants us to do this. And I have appealed for prayer. Thank God, folk have been praying for me down through the years.

Yet I think God allows us to have trouble that we might comfort others. Our suffering is for the benefit of others—"that we may be able to comfort them which are in any trouble." It is amazing how my experience with cancer has been a comfort to others. God permits us to have trouble so that we may be able to comfort others.

Listen to Paul again, "For we would not, brethren, have you ignorant of our trouble which came to us in Asia, that we were pressed out of measure, above strength, insomuch that we despaired even of life" (v. 8).

If you are as old as I am, you may remember the fable we used to have in our readers in school. The sun and the wind were having a contest to see who was the stronger. There was a man walking down the street with his coat on and the wind said, "I can make him take his coat off." So the wind began to blow. I tell you, it almost blew the man away. The harder the wind blew, the tighter the man wrapped his coat around him. The sun said, "Now it's my turn to try." The sun shone down so warm and nice that the man took his coat off. The sun accomplished what the wind could not do.

Now, generally, the wind of adversity won't take us away from God. When the wind begins to blow, when it gets rough and tough, we turn to our Father who can comfort us. However, we are in a dangerous place when things are going too well for us. When the sun is shining, Christians have it too easy. They remove that robe of practical righteousness, and they begin to compromise with the world. This is exactly what many have done in our day.

> **For our rejoicing is this, the testimony of our conscience, that in simplicity and godly sincerity, not with fleshly wisdom, but by the grace of God, we have had our conversation in the world, and more abundantly to you-ward [2 Cor. 1:12].**

"Our conversation" means our manner of life in the world. Paul says that he can rejoice because of the testimony of his life. He makes it clear that it was not by "fleshly wisdom." And, my friend, it is not by our wisdom that our lives are a testimony to those around us. If we have been a testimony for God, it is because we have lived our lives in "simplicity and godly sincerity." Paul is saying that by God's grace suffering has produced this in his life. You see, suffering is a mercy of God, and it produces qualities in our lives that are to be shared.

When I was in the hospital for my initial cancer surgery, someone sent me this little poem:

I NEEDED THE QUIET

I needed the quiet so He drew me aside,
Into the shadows where we could confide.

Away from the bustle where all the day long
I hurried and worried when active and strong.

I needed the quiet though at first I rebelled.
But gently, so gently, my cross He upheld,

And whispered so sweetly of spiritual things.
Though weakened in body, my spirit took wings

To heights never dreamed of when active and gay.
He loved me so greatly He drew me away.

I needed the quiet. No prison my bed,
But a beautiful valley of blessings instead—

A place to grow richer in Jesus to hide.
I needed the quiet so He drew me aside.
                    —Alice Hansche Mortenson

My friend, if today you are on a bed of pain, and you are in the will of God, that bed can become a greater pulpit than the one preachers stand behind.

For we write none other things unto you, than what ye read or acknowledge; and I trust ye shall acknowledge even to the end;

As also ye have acknowledged us in part, that we are your rejoicing, even as ye also are ours in the day of the Lord Jesus.

And in this confidence I was minded to come unto you before, that ye might have a second benefit [2 Cor. 1:13–15].

Paul is saying, "Wasn't I a blessing to you the first time? Now I am coming a second time, and I want to be a blessing to you."

> **And to pass by you into Macedonia, and to come again out of Macedonia unto you, and of you to be brought on my way toward Judaea.**

> **When I therefore was thus minded, did I use lightness? or the things that I purpose, do I purpose according to the flesh, that with me there should be yea yea, and nay nay? [2 Cor. 1:16–17].**

Paul had hoped that he would be able to come to Corinth, but he hadn't come there yet. Some of his enemies in Corinth were saying that he didn't mean what he said. They accused him of being insincere. Now Paul is telling them that he certainly was sincere. He says that when he says yes, he means yes, and when he says no, he means no.

Believers today ought to be that kind of folk. They should not use lightness in making appointments and arrangements in the business world and in their daily appointments. We need Christian men and women who will stand by the things that they have said.

> **But as God is true, our word toward you was not yea and nay [2 Cor. 1:18].**

Paul didn't say, "I will come," then, "I won't come"—as though he was being fickle. Why? Because *God* had led him. He was in the will of *God*.

> **For the Son of God, Jesus Christ, who was preached among you by us, even by me and Silvanus and Timotheus, was not yea and nay, but in him was yea [2 Cor. 1:19].**

The gospel that he had preached was a glorious, positive gospel, and it was "yea." The gospel is something God has done for us—it is good news. We have not only the faithful God, but the sure Lord Jesus Christ.

> **For all the promises of God in him are yea, and in him Amen, unto the glory of God by us [2 Cor. 1:20].**

Everything is positive in Christ. You see, God means well by you, Christian friend.

> **Now he which stablisheth us with you in Christ, and hath anointed us, is God;**
>
> **Who hath also sealed us, and given the earnest of the Spirit in our hearts [2 Cor. 1:21–22].**

Now you have here not only the faithful God, the true God, and the sure Lord Jesus, but you have the indwelling Holy Spirit. And I believe, very candidly, that you have here in this statement the total ministry of the Holy Spirit today.

"He which stablisheth us." Now how do you become established? When Paul had written his first letter to these Corinthians—and they had been so fickle—he concluded by saying, ". . . be ye stedfast, unmoveable, always abounding in the work of the Lord, forasmuch as ye know that your labour is not in vain in the Lord" (1 Cor. 15:58). What does it mean to be established? We believe that is the work of the Holy Spirit. First of all, the Holy Spirit convicts. The Lord Jesus said that when the Holy Spirit came into the world, He would convict the world of sin, righteousness, and judgment. And the second thing that He would do (if, having been convicted, we confessed our sin and accepted Christ as our Savior) would be to regenerate us, you see. And He not only would regenerate us, He would indwell us. And not only would He indwell us, but He would baptize us.

And by the way, this expression here is quite interesting: "Now he which stablisheth us with you in [into] Christ, and hath anointed us, is *God*." God who? God the Holy Spirit, if you please.

Sometimes, especially at funerals, we hear the song, "Safe in the

Arms of Jesus." Well, the word here is not safe *in* the arms of Jesus. When you are put into Christ by the baptism of the Holy Spirit, you are a part of His body. Rather than being safe *in* His arms, you are as safe *as* an arm of Jesus Christ. You are as safe as a member of His body. What a wonderful security that is!

In speaking of the work of the Holy Spirit, Paul uses the present tense. This is what He is doing for you today, my friend: He convicts you, He regenerates you, He indwells you, and He baptizes you.

"Now he which . . . hath anointed us, is God." The anointing of the Holy Spirit is a neglected truth in our day. In 1 John 2:20 we are told, "But ye have an unction [that is, an *anointing*] from the Holy One, and ye know all things." That anointing is the Holy Spirit. It takes the Holy Spirit to lead and guide us into all truth. "But the anointing which ye have received of him abideth in you, and ye need not that any man teach you: but as the same anointing teacheth you of all things, and is truth, and is no lie, and even as it hath taught you, ye shall abide in him" (1 John 2:27). This ministry of the Holy Spirit is very important. He doesn't give you a mail-order degree, nor does this knowledge come in a gift-wrapped box. You have the Holy Spirit to teach you, Christian friend, and He alone can open the Word of God to you. That is the reason this is a miracle Book. The Lord Jesus said to His own men, "I have yet many things to say unto you, but ye cannot bear them now. Howbeit when he, the Spirit of truth, is come, he will guide you into all truth . . ." (John 16:12–13). He *wants* to guide you into all truth.

"Who hath also sealed us"—that is a marvelous ministry of the Spirit. "And grieve not the holy Spirit of God, whereby ye are sealed unto the day of redemption" (Eph. 4:30). Is it possible to grieve Him away? No, He has sealed us and is going to deliver us someday. This is somewhat like taking a letter down to the post office. Occasionally some of the mail is lost and never does get delivered. If we want to be very sure that a certain piece of mail arrives, we have that letter registered and a seal put on it. The postal service guarantees that they will get the letter to the person to whom it is addressed. Also, all legal documents bear a seal—"In witness thereof I set my seal" is the phraseology that has come down to us from old English. It is also a brand, a mark of ownership. In the early days of the West, when there were no fences, the cattlemen would brand their cattle. The brand was a mark of ownership.

The Holy Spirit puts a brand on you to show that you belong to God. My friend, if you are little sheep of His, you are not going to get lost. Oh, you may stray away, but He will come to find you. The Holy Spirit is pictured in Luke's parable as the woman sweeping the floor, looking for the lost coin until she *found* it (see Luke 15:8).

"And given the earnest of the Spirit in our hearts" would be better translated: you are "given the earnest, which is the Holy Spirit in our hearts." You know that "earnest money" indicates there will be more to follow. When you put down earnest money on a piece of property, it is a pledge that you are going to pay more money on that property. In such a way, God has given us the Holy Spirit, which indicates there is more to follow. This is a wonderful thing.

When people buy on the installment plan, there is a possibility that the buyer may later defect, even though he has put a down payment on the merchandise. But there is no defection in this Buyer. He has purchased us with His blood. He has put down a purchase price, which guarantees that the saved soul will be delivered safely to the Father. It means that the saved soul is in escrow today.

God has put His Holy Spirit into every believer. He is the earnest. He has come into the life of the believer to bring the fullness of God to bear in our experiences. What is it that you need today? You know that He is rich in mercy—He is the Father of mercies. What do you need? Why don't you go to Him and ask Him for it? Do you need power? Do you need joy? Do you need wisdom? Do you need help? These are comforts—He is the God of all comfort. Paul knew this; he had experienced it. Also, the writer knows it; he has *experienced* it.

> **Moreover I call God for a record upon my soul, that to spare you I came not as yet unto Corinth [2 Cor. 1:23].**

Paul says that if he had come earlier, he would have done what he did in his first epistle. You have seen that 1 Corinthians is filled with correction. Paul was really stern in that epistle. In effect, he is saying, "If

I had come, I would have been stern with you. But I wanted to spare you that; I wanted to see if you would work this thing out yourselves."

Not for that we have dominion over your faith, but are helpers of your joy: for by faith ye stand [2 Cor. 1:24].

Paul is saying, "I am not the bishop of your souls. I am not trying to lord it over you. You have complete freedom in Christ. I just want to be a helper of your joy; 'for by faith ye stand.'" You and I too must stand in our own faith, my friend. Paul stayed away so that their faith might be strengthened and that they might grow in the Lord. And this is one of the reasons God permits many of us to undergo certain hardships and certain difficulties in our lives.

CHAPTER 2

THEME: God's comfort in restoring a sinning saint

This epistle is teaching us wonderful truths about God's comfort. In the first chapter we saw God's comfort for life's plans. Now we see God's comfort in restoring a sinning saint. Before the apostle gets into this subject, he continues with the subject of chapter 1. He is explaining his motives for not coming for an earlier visit. Then he discusses the sinning saint in the congregation in Corinth. Finally, he shows that God causes us to triumph in Christ.

PAUL'S EXPLANATION CONTINUES

But I determined this with myself, that I would not come again to you in heaviness [2 Cor. 2:1].

Paul admits that he was discouraged with them. If he had come to visit them, it would have been in sorrow.

For if I make you sorry, who is he then that maketh me glad, but the same which is made sorry by me? [2 Cor. 2:2].

Paul didn't want to come in his sorrow, with tears in his eyes. He would have had them weeping, too. Then who would make Paul glad? They would all have been boo-hooing into their handkerchiefs.

And I wrote this same unto you, lest, when I came, I should have sorrow from them of whom I ought to rejoice; having confidence in you all, that my joy is the joy of you all [2 Cor. 2:3].

Paul wanted to come to them in joy. He had been hoping to get word from them telling him that they had corrected those things about which he had written them.

Now Paul opens his heart to them.

> **For out of much affliction and anguish of heart I wrote unto you with many tears; not that ye should be grieved, but that ye might know the love which I have more abundantly unto you [2 Cor. 2:4].**

A great many people today fall out with the preacher when he preaches a message that is rather severe. Sometimes correction from the Word of God will really bear down on the congregation. Some people think that a pastor should not do that. May I say to you, my friend, that a faithful pastor *must* do that. The command is: "I charge thee therefore before God, and the Lord Jesus Christ, who shall judge the quick and the dead at his appearing and his kingdom; Preach the word; be instant in season, out of season; reprove, rebuke, exhort with all longsuffering and doctrine" (2 Tim. 4:1–2). Any man who stands in the pulpit today has a tremendous responsibility to rebuke what is wrong. Many of the saints don't like this. Paul tells them here that his rebuke was not because he was opposed to them, but because he loved them. A faithful pastor shows his love by preaching the Word of God as it is rather than "buttering up" the congregation.

RESTORING A SINNING SAINT

Let me remind you that in Paul's first letter to the Corinthian church, he rebuked them because they were permitting gross immorality in the congregation. In fact, they had a case of incest in their congregation, and they were shutting their eyes to it. (Yet they were acting as if they were very spiritual!) This kind of gross immorality was something that was even shocking to the heathen; yet the congregation was ignoring it. Paul had written them to get this matter straightened out. He read the riot act to them. He told them, ". . . put away from among yourselves that wicked person" (1 Cor. 5:13).

The congregation did listen to Paul. They excommunicated the man.

> **But if any have caused grief, he hath not grieved me, but in part: that I may not overcharge you all.**
>
> **Sufficient to such a man is this punishment, which was inflicted of many [2 Cor. 2:5–6].**

They had obeyed Paul. They had excommunicated the man, which was the right thing for them to do.

Then the man acknowledged his sin and came under great conviction. Now what ought they to do? They should forgive him.

> **So that contrariwise ye ought rather to forgive him, and comfort him, lest perhaps such a one should be swallowed up with overmuch sorrow.**
>
> **Wherefore I beseech you that ye would confirm your love toward him [2 Cor. 2:7–8].**

"He will be overwhelmed, not only because of his sin, but because you won't receive him. So now put your arm about him, and restore him to your fellowship." To the Galatian believers Paul wrote: "Brethren, if a man be overtaken in a fault, ye which are spiritual, restore such an one in the spirit of meekness; considering thyself, lest thou also be tempted" (Gal. 6:1).

> **For to this end also did I write, that I might know the proof of you, whether ye be obedient in all things.**
>
> **To whom ye forgive any thing, I forgive also: for if I forgave any thing, to whom I forgave it, for your sakes forgave I it in the person of Christ;**
>
> **Lest Satan should get an advantage of us; for we are not ignorant of his devices [2 Cor. 2:9–11].**

You see, the Devil tries to push us one way or another. Sometimes the Devil gets us to shut our eyes to gross immorality. There are many instances of that in our churches today. I know one preacher who has had trouble with women in three different churches. Each church he went to serve knew his past record, and still they accepted him as pastor! In shutting their eyes to gross immorality, they were hurting the cause of Christ Jesus.

Now suppose he had repented and had really turned from his sin (which he did not), then they should have forgiven him. Unfortunately, many of our stiff-backed brethren will not forgive anything. That can be the work of the Devil as well as shutting one's eyes to immorality. Satan gets the advantage of a great many Christians because they are unforgiving. There are two things that we don't hear very often even in our conservative churches: we don't hear folk admitting their sins and asking for forgiveness nor do we hear folk forgiving those who confess. There is an unforgiving spirit in many of our churches.

We need to remember that we are all capable of any sin. Whatever the other man has done, we are also capable of doing. When such a man repents from his sin, he is to be restored in the spirit of meekness. He is to be brought back into fellowship. This is part of the ministry. It is a glorious ministry, isn't it?

> **Furthermore, when I came to Troas to preach Christ's gospel, and a door was opened unto me of the Lord [2 Cor. 2:12].**

He came to Troas, and there he found an open door. It was the will of God for him to stay there and to preach the gospel rather than proceed on to Corinth at that time. Paul was not being fickle. He was being faithful. He was faithful to the opportunity which God gave him.

> **I had no rest in my spirit, because I found not Titus my brother: but taking my leave of them, I went from thence into Macedonia [2 Cor. 2:13].**

Even while he was preaching the gospel in Troas, he was grieved at heart because Titus hadn't come to bring him word concerning the congregation in Corinth. He waited for Titus to come, but Titus didn't come. Then Paul went over to Philippi in Macedonia. It was there that Titus came and brought word that the Corinthians had dealt with this sin in their congregation and that the man had now repented and had turned from his sin.

THE TRIUMPHANT MINISTRY

Now we come to what some have called the power of the ministry. It is part of the greatness of the ministry, and I rejoice today to be able to preach the kind of gospel and the kind of Word of God that we have to give. We are dealing here with a grand and glorious picture.

Now thanks be unto God, which always causeth us to triumph in Christ, and maketh manifest the savour of his knowledge by us in every place [2 Cor. 2:14].

In this dramatic picture, Paul is saying that preaching the gospel is like leading a triumphal entry. The background is a Roman triumphal entry. One of the great Roman generals would go out to the frontier—to Europe where my ancestors were at that time, or down into Africa—where he would have victory after victory, for Rome was victorious in most campaigns. The conqueror would then return to Rome, and there would be a big, triumphal entry into the city. It is said that sometimes the triumphal entry would begin in the morning and go on far into the night. The Roman conqueror would be bringing in animals and other booty which he had captured. In the front of the procession would be the people who were going to be released. They had been captured but would be freed and would become Roman citizens. In the back of the procession would be the captive people who were to be executed.

In these triumphal entries there was always the burning of incense. They would be burning the incense to their gods to whom they gave credit for the victory. All the way through the procession would be clouds of smoke from the incense, sometimes even obscuring the procession as it passed by.

With this as a background, Paul is saying, "Thanks be unto God, which always causeth us to triumph in Christ." This is wonderful, friend. You can't lose when you are in Christ. You cannot lose! Paul says that God *always* causeth us to triumph. Wait a minute, Paul. Always? In every place? We know you had wonderful success in Ephesus, but you didn't do so well in Athens. Do you feel that you triumphed in both places? "Yes," Paul says, "He always causes us to triumph in Christ!"

"And maketh manifest the savour [the sweet incense] of his knowledge by us in every place." Are you having a victory when no one turns to Christ? "Oh, yes," Paul says.

> **For we are unto God a sweet savour of Christ, in them that are saved, and in them that perish [2 Cor. 2:15].**

In that triumphal entry were those who were going to be set free and those who were going to be executed—but all of them were in the triumphal entry.

> **To the one we are the savour of death unto death; and to the other the savour of life unto life. And who is sufficient for these things? [2 Cor. 2:16].**

Paul is overwhelmed by this—"who is sufficient for these things?" My friend, the greatest privilege in the world is to give out the Word of God. There is nothing like it. I would never want to run for the presidency of the United States. It is difficult to understand why anyone would want to be president in this day of unsolvable problems. But it is glorious to give out the Word of God! Do you know why? Because He always causes us to triumph!

While I was a pastor in Los Angeles, we very seldom had a Sunday when someone didn't turn to Christ, and many times there were a great many folk.

When the gospel is preached and the multitudes accept Christ, that is wonderful. We can see the triumph there. We are a "savour of life" unto those who are saved. But now wait a minute—what about the crowd which rejects Christ? We are a "savour of death" to them. I often say to the congregation after I have preached a message, "If you go out of here after rejecting Christ, I am probably the worst enemy you will ever have, because now you cannot go into the presence of God and say that you never heard the gospel." However, all people are now in the triumphal entry. Many will not be set free; they will be judged. But regardless of our destiny, we are in the great triumphal entry of Jesus Christ because He is going to *win*, my friend! Every knee must bow to him, and every tongue shall confess that Jesus Christ is Lord. Every individual will have to bow to Him someday— regardless of whether He is the person's Savior or Judge. No wonder Paul exclaims, "Who is sufficient for these things?"

"To the one we are the savour of death unto death; and to the other the savour of life unto life." Today the incense is ascending; the Word is going out. And we are a savor of life to some and a savor of death to others.

For we are not as many, which corrupt the word of God: but as of sincerity, but as of God, in the sight of God speak we in Christ [2 Cor. 2:17].

This is the entire plan of the Christian ministry. We are not to corrupt the Word of God or distort it or make merchandise of it, but to give it out in sincerity as the Spirit of God reveals its truth to us.

CHAPTER 3

THEME: *God's comfort in the glorious ministry of Christ*

Paul has spoken of the triumph of the ministry. Now he deals with the accreditation of the ministry. He will reach the heights in this chapter.

> **Do we begin again to commend ourselves? or need we, as some others, epistles of commendation to you, or letters of commendation from you? [2 Cor. 3:1].**

Paul is asking, "Do I need a letter of recommendation from my employer? Do I need a letter from God testifying that I am His minister?" Paul says, "No, I don't need to have that"—for this reason:

> **Ye are our epistle written in our hearts, known and read of all men:**

> **Forasmuch as ye are manifestly declared to be the epistle of Christ ministered by us, written not with ink, but with the Spirit of the living God; not in tables of stone, but in fleshy tables of the heart [2 Cor. 3:2–3].**

The proof of the effectiveness of any ministry is whether or not it has a recommendation from God. He is not giving out letters of recommendation; the proof lies in the epistles that are written in the fleshly tables of the heart. I read many letters from folk who have turned to Christ because of my radio ministry. Several years ago a wonderful family came up to me in Houston, Texas. If no one else turned to Christ through my radio program there, I still would consider it worthwhile. They listened to the radio program for three months before they made a decision for Christ, and then the entire family, a handsome family, all received Christ. They are some of the epistles I have down in Texas. I have such epistles in practically every state of these United States and on many foreign shores. They are my letters of commendation.

Paul says to the Corinthian believers, "You are our epistles written in our hearts, known and read of all men."

> **And such trust have we through Christ to God-ward [2 Cor. 3:4].**

This gives me confidence. I know the Bible is the Word of God. When I was in seminary, I believed it was the Word of God. I think that intellectually it can be determined that it is the Word of God. But today I don't even need the intellectual demonstrations anymore. I've passed that. To me it is very simple—the proof of the Word of God is what it does. They say that the proof of the pudding is in the eating. God put it like this: "O taste and see that the LORD is good . . ." (Ps. 34:8). This is His challenge to you.

> **Not that we are sufficient of ourselves to think any thing as of ourselves; but our sufficiency is of God [2 Cor. 3:5].**

I am sure that you have already sensed the weakness of the apostle Paul in this epistle of 2 Corinthians. But Paul could say, "For when I am weak, then am I strong" (2 Cor. 12:10).

God is not looking for some big something or some big somebody. If He had wanted that, He couldn't use me and He couldn't use you. God chooses the weak things of this world, little things, insignificant things to accomplish His purposes. Our sufficiency is of God.

CONTRASTS BETWEEN THE OLD AND NEW COVENANTS

> **Who also hath made us able ministers of the new testament; not of the letter, but of the spirit: for the letter killeth, but the spirit giveth life [2 Cor. 3:6].**

We are ministers "of the new testament" would be better translated, ministers of the new *covenant*. We will see a contrast between the old covenant (the Old Testament) and the new covenant (the New Testament). There is a contrast here in several different ways.

"Not of the letter, but of the spirit." In the Old Testament, and specifically in the Law, the letter kills; the letter of the Law actually condemns us. The Law says that you and I are guilty sinners. Those letters which were written on the tablets of stone condemned man. The Mosaic Law never gave life. That is the contrast he is making here. The letter kills. "For the letter killeth, but the spirit giveth life."

I have often challenged congregations to name somebody who was saved by the Law. Did you know that even Moses, the law-giver, could not be saved by the Law? Do you know why not? He was a murderer! Also David broke the Law even though he was a man after God's own heart. Friend, you can't be saved by keeping the Law. The Law kills you; the Law condemns you.

> **But if the ministration of death, written and engraven in stones, was glorious, so that the children of Israel could not stedfastly behold the face of Moses for the glory of his countenance; which glory was to be done away [2 Cor. 3:7].**

The old covenant, the Law, was a ministration of death. When it says that it was written and engraved on stones, we know he is talking about the Ten Commandments.

It "was glorious." It is the will of God, and it is good, even though it condemns me. There is nothing wrong with the Law. The problem is with me. It shows me that I am a sinner. "So that the children of Israel could not stedfastly behold the face of Moses for the glory of his countenance; which glory was to be done away." That glory on Moses' face slowly disappeared.

> **How shall not the ministration of the spirit be rather glorious? [2 Cor. 3:8].**

If the Old Testament was glorious, how much more the New Testament!

> **For if the ministration of condemnation be glory, much more doth the ministration of righteousness exceed in glory [2 Cor. 3:9].**

"The ministration of righteousness" is the righteousness which we have in Christ Jesus.

> **For even that which was made glorious had no glory in this respect, by reason of the glory that excelleth.**
>
> **For if that which is done away was glorious, much more that which remaineth is glorious [2 Cor. 3:10–11].**

"That which is done away" is the Law. Notice that it *is* "done away." Then how much more glorious is that which remains, that new covenant. He is making a contrast between the giving of the Mosaic Law and the day of grace in which we live.

> **Seeing then that we have such hope, we use great plainness of speech:**
>
> **And not as Moses, which put a veil over his face, that the children of Israel could not stedfastly look to the end of that which is abolished [2 Cor. 3:12–13].**

To what is he having reference?

We need to recognize that there was a first giving and a second giving of the Law. When Moses went to the top of Mount Sinai, God gave him the tablets of stone, and God Himself wrote the Law on them. That was the Law that the children of Israel were to live by and actually be saved by (if they could keep it—which no one could). And they were going to be judged by it. While Moses was up on the mountain with God, the children of Israel were already breaking the first two commandments: "Thou shalt have no other gods before me"

(Exod. 20:3) and "Thou shalt not make unto thee any graven image . . ." (Exod. 20:4). The Mosaic Law was a very strict, rigid law. Even Moses said, ". . . I exceedingly fear and quake" (Heb. 12:21). It demanded an eye for an eye, a tooth for a tooth, burning for burning, and cutting for cutting. It was absolute, intrinsic righteousness and holiness. Whatever a man deserved according to the Law that was what he was to receive. In Exodus 32 the people were already breaking the Law. What is going to happen? God told Moses to go down to the people. When Moses went down the mountain, he could see from a distance that the children of Israel were breaking the first two commandments, and he didn't dare bring the tables of the Law into the camp. Why not? If he had, the entire nation of Israel would have been blotted out at that very moment. They would have been judged immediately because the breaking of those laws meant instant death. So Moses smashed those tablets of stone; then he went into the camp.

Now when Moses goes back to the top of Mount Sinai into the presence of God, we see that something happens. Moses recognizes that all Israel should be destroyed because of their sin, but he asks God for mercy. And God gives them a second chance as He gives Moses the second tables of the Law. Moses now understands that God is tempering the Law with mercy and grace. At the very heart of the Mosaic system is to be a tabernacle and a sacrificial system that will be the basis of approach to God, which is ". . . without shedding of blood [there] is no remission" of sin (Heb. 9:22). But "without holiness, no man is going to see God" (see Heb. 12:14). How in the world are we going to get into His presence? Well, God will have to make a way for us, and God did make a way. What a glorious, wonderful revelation this is. No wonder Moses' face shone!

When Moses came down from the mount, he had the second tables of the Law, which was a ministration of condemnation and a ministration of death, demanding a righteousness of man which he was unable to produce of himself; but also there was the sacrificial system that manifested the grace of God. It was the grace of God, fulfilled in the death and resurrection of Christ, that Paul the apostle found— Paul, who had been a man under the Law, a Pharisee of the Pharisees—and that brought him to the place where he could say,

"And be found in him [Jesus], not having mine own righteousness, which is of the law, but that which is through the faith of Christ, the righteousness which is of God by faith" (Phil. 3:9). Now here is a ministration of glory indeed, and this is the glorious gospel.

The Law was glorious. It offered man a way of salvation, but man was too feeble to fulfill its demands. It was a glorious way of life that was pleasing to God, but for man it became a ministration of death because of his lost condition.

However, the glory of the grace of God fulfilled in Christ is a ministration of glory indeed! In another passage it is called "the glorious gospel of the blessed God." The word *blessed* means "happy"—the happy God. What is it that makes God happy? The thing that makes God happy is that He is a lover of men and He delights in mercy. He wants to save man. We are told in Micah 7:18: "Who is a God like unto thee, that pardoneth iniquity, and passeth by the transgression of the remnant of his heritage? he retaineth not his anger for ever, because he delighteth in mercy." It is not God's will that any of the human family should be lost. To the prophet Ezekiel God said, "Say unto them, As I live, saith the Lord God, I have no pleasure in the death of the wicked; but that the wicked turn from his way and live: turn ye, turn ye from your evil ways; for why will ye die, O house of Israel?" (Ezek. 33:11). God wants to save—saving man is the thing that makes Him happy. We have a happy God. What a glorious picture this gives us.

When Moses came down from the mountain the second time, there was *joy* in his heart and his face *shone*. Now there was a way for the children of Israel to come into the presence of God through the sacrificial system.

Now let's make this very clear again that the veil Moses put on his face was not because his face was shining with a glory so that they couldn't look at him. It was because that glory was beginning to fade away. The fact that Moses' face shone was a glorious thing, but the glory began to fade.

**But their minds were blinded: for until this day re-
maineth the same veil untaken away in the reading of**

**the old testament; which veil is done away in Christ
[2 Cor. 3:14].**

Their minds are blinded until this very day.

The veil that Moses wore on his face is now a veil on the minds of God's ancient people. It is still there because of the fact that these people actually do not see that Christ is the end of the Law for righteousness. They do not see that *He* is the fulfillment of the whole Law. The blindness is still there.

When we get into the next chapter, we will find that the "god of this world" has blinded the minds of those who do not believe, and we will see why this is true.

**But even unto this day, when Moses is read, the veil is
upon their heart [2 Cor. 3:15].**

When they read the Law, they actually think that they are able to keep it. But in reading the Old Testament we do not find the confidence that you would expect in the hearts and minds of God's people. Even David raised some questions. Job was in absolute bewilderment. Hezekiah turned his face to the wall and wept when he faced death. However, in this day of grace in which you and I live, even the weakest saint who trusts Jesus has absolute assurance of his perfect acceptance with God.

**Nevertheless when it shall turn to the Lord, the veil shall
be taken away [2 Cor. 3:16].**

"It" refers to the heart. When the heart turns to the Lord Jesus Christ, the veil is taken away. Man's trouble is heart trouble. He is blinded because of the sin in his life. When he is willing to turn from his sin and receive the Lord Jesus as his Savior, "the veil shall be taken away."

**Now the Lord is that Spirit: and where the Spirit of the
Lord is, there is liberty [2 Cor. 3:17].**

Only the Spirit of God can lift the veil and help us to see that Christ is the Savior. He alone can do that. He is the One and the *only* One.

You notice that Paul here is saying the very same thing which Simon Peter had said: "To him give all the prophets witness, that through his name whosoever believeth in him shall receive remission of sins" (Acts 10:43). My friend, if you do not see the Lord Jesus Christ in the Old Testament, the Spirit of God takes the things of Christ and shows them unto us. The Spirit of God brings you into the place of liberty. He doesn't put you under law. He delivers you from law and brings you to Christ. When He does—

But we all, with open face beholding as in a glass the glory of the Lord, are changed into the same image from glory to glory, even as by the Spirit of the Lord [2 Cor. 3:18].

This is a very wonderful passage of Scripture. Paul has been talking about the veil being on the heart; then when we turn to Christ, that veil is taken away. Now as believers we are looking upon the Lord Jesus Christ—but even as believers our eyes are veiled when there is sin in our lives. But when that sin is confessed, and we are in fellowship with Him, we look to Him. Then we, with "open face" or unveiled face, beholding (not *reflecting* as another version translates it) as in a mirror the glory of the Lord—the idea is not of reflecting in order to transform, but rather that of beholding *until* transformed. Then we can reflect His image. I feel that a more accurate translation is: we "beholding as in a mirror the glory of the Lord, are *transformed* into the same image from glory to glory, even as from the Lord, the Spirit."

Frances E. Siewert, who lived here in Southern California in Sierra Madre, worked on The Amplified Bible. When she was still alive, she and I used to carry on a friendly battle. She would hear me on the radio and sometimes when I referred to her amplified version, I would question some things. She was a brilliant woman, and I want to be very frank and say that I lost most of the battles. However, I won a friendly battle over this verse. Let me quote this verse to you from her earliest amplified version. "And all of us, as with unveiled face, [because we] continue to behold [in the Word of God] as in a mirror the glory of the Lord, are constantly being transfigured into His very own image in ever increasing splendor *and* from one degree of glory to another; [for this comes] from the Lord [Who is] the Spirit." This is an excellent translation except for the word *transfigured*. Only the Lord Jesus was transfigured—I've never seen a saint yet that I thought had been transfigured. It is true that the Word of God is the mirror that we are to look at, and we are beholding Him—just looking at Christ. That is the reason we need to stay in the Word of God and behold the Lord Jesus. As you behold Him, you are transformed. In other words, the Word of God does more than regenerate you (we are regenerated by the Spirit of God using the Word of God). "Being born again, not of corruptible seed, but of incorruptible, by the word of God, which liveth and abideth for ever" (1 Pet. 1:23). Also the Word of God transforms us. Oh, this is so important! I wish I had spent more time looking in the mirror, beholding Him more. My friend, in the Word of God we see Him. He is not a super star; He is not just a man. In the Word of God we see the unveiled *Christ*. Oh, how wonderful He is!

Dr. H. A. Ironside told the story about an old Scot who lay suffering and, actually, dying. The physician told him he didn't have very long to live. A friend came to spend a little time with him and said to him, "They tell me you'll not be with us long." That's a nice thing to say to a man who is dying. Then he continued, "I hope you get a wee glimpse of the Savior's blessed face as you are going through the valley of the shadow." The dying man looked up when he gathered a little strength and answered, "Away with the glimpse, mon; it's a full view of His blessed face I've had these forty years, and I'll not be satisfied with any of your wee glimpses now." How wonderful to behold Him today.

Perhaps some of you remember Nathaniel Hawthorne's story about the great stone face. A little lad lived in a village where there was a mountain with a rock formation which they called the great stone face. The people had a legend that someday someone would come to the village who would look like the great stone face. He would do wonderful things for the village and be a means of great blessing. That story really took hold of the lad. During his lifetime he would gaze at the great stone face at every opportunity that he had, and he would dream of the time someone looking like the great stone face would come to the village. Years passed and as time went by, he became a young man, then an old man. He was tottering down the street one day when someone looked up and saw him coming and shouted, "He has come. The one who looks like the great stone face is here." This man had looked at the great stone face for so long that now he bore its image.

Listen to me. Do you want to be Christlike? Then spend time looking at Jesus. I recall that Dr. Lewis Sperry Chafer at the Dallas Theological Seminary used to stop us when we would sing the song, "Take time to be holy, speak oft with thy Lord" by William D. Longstaff. He would say, "Change that first line. Let us sing 'Take time to *behold* Him.'" Do you want to be holy? Then behold Him.

> Turn your eyes upon Jesus;
> Look full in His wonderful face;
> And the things of earth will grow strangely dim
> In the light of His glory and grace.

I need this. I hope you, too, sense a need of seeing Jesus Christ on the pages of the Word of God so that you might grow more like Him.

CHAPTER 4

THEME: *God's comfort in the ministry of suffering for Christ*

Here we have another facet of God's comfort. We have seen God's comfort for life's plans in chapter 1. Then in chapter 2 it was God's comfort in restoring sinning saints. Chapter 3 showed God's comfort in the glorious ministry of Christ—wasn't that third chapter wonderful? Now we are not going to come down from the mountain, but we are going to stay right up there as we see God's comfort in the ministry of suffering for Christ. We may even have to climb a little higher, and I'm not sure but what we may get into an atmosphere where I really have difficulty in breathing. Paul says, "Come up higher," and that's what we want to do.

> **Therefore seeing we have this ministry, as we have received mercy, we faint not [2 Cor. 4:1].**

This is a glorious ministry. God has given to us a message which no man could have conceived. It would be impossible for a man to work out such a plan as the gospel presents. I don't know why God allowed me to be a minister of the glorious gospel other than because of His mercy. We have seen before that God is *rich* in mercy. God did not exhaust His mercy before He got to me, because He saw that I would need a whole lot of it. He has been rich in mercy to me. By mercy He has permitted me to have a Bible-teaching radio program. Since it is by His mercy, we faint not. We rejoice in it!

What is so wonderful about this ministry? I'll tell you what is wonderful about it. When I was in seminary, I studied religions. In fact, they so fascinated me that in the first few years of my ministry I almost decided to specialize in the field of comparative religions. Although I didn't do that, I am acquainted with quite a few religions of the world. It is very simply expressed by one word. All the religions of the world say, "Do, do, do." The gospel says, "Done." The gospel tells me that God has done something for me; I am to believe it; I am to trust Him. The only way I can come to Him is by faith. That is my approach to Him. "But without faith it is impossible to please him . . ." (Heb. 11:6). In contrast to this, the religions of this world all say, "Do." It is almost amusing to see what the cults in this country say one must do to be right with God. One cult declares there are four things, one of them says there are seven things you must do, another has ten things you must do—the Ten Commandments.

Some of these cults say you must have faith. However, by "faith" they do not mean a trust in Jesus Christ, but rather an acknowledgment as historical fact that Jesus lived and that He died over nineteen hundred years ago. May I say to you, it will not save you simply to believe that Jesus died. My friend, Jesus Christ died *for* our *sins* and rose again, according to the Scriptures. That is the important distinction. In His finished work we must put our trust. It is done.

At one time Paul had been under the Law. He knew what it was to be under a system of "do, do, do." He says he was "an Hebrew of the Hebrews; as touching the law, a Pharisee . . . touching the righteousness which is in the law, blameless" (Phil. 3:5–6). He was really under the Law, and he hoped that he would be able to work out his salvation. Then one day he met the Lord Jesus Christ on the Damascus road. After he came to know Him as Lord and Savior, he wrote, "That I may . . . be found in him, not having mine own righteousness, which is of the law, but that which is through the faith of Christ, the righteousness which is of God by faith" (Phil. 3:8–9). You see, after Paul had stood in the presence of Jesus Christ, he saw that he could never make it on his own. Any righteousness he might have by the Law would not be enough. He would need to have the righteousness of Christ. Paul says that was a new day for him.

It is a new day for each of us when we recognize this fact. Today we need mercy. God has been merciful; God loved us. God in His mercy provided a Savior for us, and now He saves us by His grace. How wonderful He is!

But have renounced the hidden things of dishonesty, not walking in craftiness, nor handling the word of God de-

ceitfully; but by manifestation of the truth commending ourselves to every man's conscience in the sight of God [2 Cor. 4:2].

We are saved by the grace of God through faith in Christ Jesus. However, after we have been saved, that gospel must live in us. We have renounced the hidden things of dishonesty. Coming to Christ and trusting Him is more than an intellectual assent to the fact that Christ died on the Cross. It is placing our *trust* in Him and experiencing His regeneration. When Christ has saved us, we ought to be an example of the gospel. In other words, the man who preaches the gospel should be a holy man. Paul says that we have "renounced the hidden things of dishonesty."

The translation of this verse from *The Amplified Bible* is very good, and it brings out all the facets of these words which Paul uses in this verse. Compare your Bible with this version: "We have renounced disgraceful ways—secret thoughts, feelings, desires and underhandedness, methods and arts that men hid through shame; we refuse to deal craftily (to practice trickery and cunning) or to adulterate or handle dishonestly the Word of God; but we state the truth openly—clearly and candidly. And so we commend ourselves in the sight and presence of God to every man's conscience."

We are not to walk in hypocrisy. We should not be unreal. Our behavior should not contradict that which we are preaching. It ought to be a conduct which meets the approval of the Lord Jesus Christ. We are not perfect, but we are to walk in a way that is well pleasing to Him.

We are not to handle "the word of God deceitfully." We are not to be huckstering the Word of God. This gets right down to where we live. Mr. Preacher, why do you preach? Are you preaching for money? You say that you preach for the love of souls, but is it really the love of souls? Or is it for money? I need to examine my own heart on this score. Paul wrote ". . . woe is unto me, if I preach not the gospel!" (1 Cor. 9:16).

A person can preach the gospel and say things that are absolutely true, but at the same time his life can be speaking another message. I pray a great deal about this in my own life. I pray, "O God, don't let me preach unless I can have a clear conscience, and unless I am preaching in the power of the Spirit of God." I don't want to preach unless there are those two things. It is a glorious thing to preach the gospel, but it is an awful thing to preach it if down underneath there is a lack of sincerity, a lack of being committed to Him and having a conviction about Him.

Actually, this is directed to the Christian layman. Do you want to be a witness for Christ? You are a witness either for or against Him. When Paul speaks of the ministry here, he is not referring to the clergy or the man in the pulpit, he is speaking of the man in the pew. The man in the pulpit is to train people for the work of the ministry. Our business is to help equip them for that work.

I heard a tremendous analogy the other day: Sheep produce sheep. The shepherd cannot produce sheep. He watches over the sheep. It is the sheep today who are going to win sheep, because sheep produce sheep. My business is to equip the layman to witness.

By the way, are you doing something to get out the Word of God? That is witnessing. God may have given you the gift of making money. Do you use it to send out the Word of God? Perhaps you are a man or woman of prayer, interceding for those who preach and teach the Word of God. You have contact with some person whom no one else could reach. Many people will not listen to me. They tune me in and then they tune me out. Maybe you can reach a person who will not listen to anyone else. God has called you to be a witness, my friend. This is tremendous!

But if our gospel be hid, it is hid to them that are lost:

In whom the god of this world hath blinded the minds of them which believe not, lest the light of the glorious gospel of Christ, who is the image of God, should shine unto them [2 Cor. 4:3–4].

"The god of this world" should be translated "the god of this *age*." I don't like to hear Satan called the god of this *world*. One fall Mrs.

McGee and I had the privilege of driving through eastern Ohio, West Virginia, Pennsylvania, and Maryland, around Virginia and across into Indiana, Illinois, Missouri, and Arkansas. How beautiful it was! May I say to you that it was God's world that we were looking at. Although sin has marred it, it is still God's world.

Satan *is* the god of this age. He is running it. He runs the United Nations; he runs all the amusements; he is running the whole show as far as I can tell. He is the god of this age.

He has "blinded the minds of them which believe not." Have you ever heard someone say, "I don't understand the gospel. I have heard it all my life, but it doesn't mean anything to me"? I have heard people say that again and again. What has happened? The Devil has blinded them. The light is shining, but the Devil has blinded their eyes so they cannot see. This always reminds me of a group of miners who were trapped in a mine in West Virginia after an explosion. Finally rescuers got food over to them, and then they got an electric light over to the place where they were trapped. A young miner there was looking right into the light and said, "Why don't they turn on the lights?" All of the men looked at him, startled. He had been blinded by the explosion. Satan blinds many folk. They say, "Why don't you turn on the light? I don't see the gospel at all." That is the blindness that comes from Satan.

There are other folk who say, "There are things in the Bible that I cannot believe. I don't know why, but I just can't believe them." I had a letter the other day from a man who accused me of preaching a gospel that is not true and of knowing that the Bible is not true. Oh, what arrogance! I wrote to him that I had never read a letter in which I had seen such a display of arrogance and ignorance. But do you know what was really his problem? It was not that there are things in the Bible which he couldn't believe. The problem was that there was *sin* in his life, sin that the Bible condemns. He didn't *want* to believe. That is the condition of a lot of folk today. The problem is not with the Bible; the problem is with their lives. My friend, if you choose to go on indulging your sins, then you can go on doing that. It is your loss. But you *can* turn to Christ. Don't tell me you cannot. You can turn to Christ if you will. The moment a man comes to the place where he sees himself as a sinner and says, "I am ready to renounce my sin; I'm ready to receive Christ as my Savior," he will be saved. The Word of God is light. Instead of saying you cannot see the light and instead of trying to blame the Bible, why don't you face your sins before God? Then there will be no difficulty about your believing.

I would like to give you a quotation from Sir Isaac Newton. Certainly no one could say that he was not an intellectual or that he was not a man of remarkable ability. One day someone said this to him: "Sir Isaac, I do not understand. You seem to be able to believe the Bible like a little child. I have tried but I cannot. So many of its statements mean nothing to me. I cannot believe; I cannot understand." This was the reply of Sir Isaac Newton: "Sometimes I come into my study and in my absentmindedness I attempt to light my candle when the extinguisher is over it, and I fumble about trying to light it and cannot; but when I remove the extinguisher then I am able to light the candle. I am afraid the extinguisher in your case is the love of your sins; it is deliberate unbelief that is in you. Turn to God in repentance; be prepared to let the Spirit of God reveal His truth to you, and it will be His joy to show the glory of the grace of God shining in the face of Jesus Christ." Sir Isaac Newton was not only a great scientist but also a great preacher. Why don't people believe? Because Satan has blinded their eyes "lest the light of the glorious gospel of Christ, who is the image of God, should shine unto them." It is a glorious gospel, but it is glorious because it reveals the glory of Christ. Apparently that is what men do not want to see.

For we preach not ourselves, but Christ Jesus the Lord; and ourselves your servants for Jesus' sake [2 Cor. 4:5].

We preach Christ Jesus the Lord. Believe me, my friend, you and I are helpless when we give out the Word of God. There is an enemy opposed to us, and he blinds the minds of people.

For God, who commanded the light to shine out of darkness, hath shined in our hearts, to give the light of the

**knowledge of the glory of God in the face of Jesus Christ
[2 Cor. 4:6].**

Paul goes back to the time of creation when God created light. I don't know when creation took place. A great many folk believe that in order to be a fundamentalist one must believe that God created this universe in 4,004 B.C. I do not know any of my fundamental brethren who hold that viewpoint. Way back yonder in the beginning God created it. He did not give us the date. Our God is a God of eternity. He wasn't just sitting around twiddling His thumbs waiting for man to appear on the scene. Man is a Johnny-come-lately, of course, but God has been here a long, long, long time. I hold the position that this universe has been here for a long time and that something happened to it. It bears evidence of some titanic convulsion that took place. Something must have happened to a perfect creation. We are told in Genesis 1 that God moved in. The Spirit of God moved, or the actual word is *brooded*, upon the face of the waters. Then God said, "Let there be light," and there was light!

Now Paul tells us that God, "who commanded the light to shine out of darkness [in Genesis 1], hath shined in our hearts, to give the light of the knowledge of the glory of God in the face of Jesus Christ." Just as the Spirit of God brooded over the waters, so the Spirit of God broods over a soul. He moves in to bring conviction to our hearts. Then He regenerates us. And the light of the glorious gospel of Christ, who is the image of God, shines in. Here we are back looking at Him. As someone has said, "The look saves, but the gaze sanctifies." We need to spend a lot of time looking at Him. But even doing this, we are weak vessels.

But we have this treasure in earthen vessels, that the excellency of the power may be of God, and not of us [2 Cor. 4:7].

We are just an "earthen vessel." The picture here is a vivid one. The Greek word for "earthen" is *ostrakinos*—this is what archaeologists are digging up today. Actually, many of their diggings are in the old city dumps where all the broken pottery (clay vessels) was thrown. When I was in Lebanon, I went down to Tyre and walked along an excavation. It goes across the place where Alexander the Great filled in between the mainland and the island to form a peninsula there. I walked out on that to see the excavation going on. There was so much broken pottery there that I could have filled bushel baskets. That is how we are pictured here—weak clay vessels, pottery that can be broken.

"But we have this treasure." What is the treasure? That is the glorious gospel. We carry this glorious gospel in our little, old earthen vessels. That is why Paul says, "For we preach not ourselves, but Christ Jesus the Lord; and ourselves your servants for Jesus' sake." Sometimes we get the idea we want to be a great preacher or even a great Christian. That is one reason that I am not sure we ought to be having all these testimonies that we hear today. It is pretty easy for a man to begin to brag in his testimony. If Jesus Christ is not glorified in a testimony, there is no point in it whatsoever. After all, we are just servants. That is the best that can be said of us.

The simile of earthen vessels takes us back to the incident at the time of Gideon. In Judges 7 we read that Gideon took only three hundred men with him to free their land of innumerable Midianite invaders. Each man had a trumpet and a torch and a pitcher or an earthen vessel. They carried their torches in the earthen vessels so that the light couldn't be seen from a distance. Then when they got among the Midianites, they broke the earthen vessels. It wasn't until the earthen vessel was broken that the light could shine out.

My friend, that is the thing which we need today. We need the vessel to be broken. The apostle Paul was a man who knew what it was to suffer for Jesus' sake. That vessel had to be broken. The trouble today is that we don't have very many who are willing to do that. I remember that Dr. George Gill used to tell us this in class: "When someone is born, someone has to travail. The reason that more people are not being born again is that there are not enough who are willing to travail." We hear a great deal about witnessing today, but, my friend, what kind of a price are you willing to pay? It is not enough to just knock on a door and visit someone. I'm not minimizing that, and I'm not saying it isn't important, but I am saying that the earthen vessel must be broken. We cannot have our way *and* His way in our lives. We need to make up our minds whether we are going to follow Him or not.

We are troubled on every side, yet not distressed; we are perplexed, but not in despair [2 Cor. 4:8].

Paul is making a comparison here. He says, "We are troubled." That is a comparative degree. But he says, "Yet not distressed." That is a superlative. He was pressed for room, as it were, but he still had room to preach the gospel. There was hand-to-hand combat in the corner, but he still could turn to God.

"We are perplexed"—he was unable to find a way out—"but not in despair." He did get out—the Spirit of God led him.

Persecuted, but not forsaken; cast down, but not destroyed [2 Cor. 4:9].

He was "persecuted," pursued by enemies, but he was "not forsaken"—he was not overtaken by the enemies. When he was in prison, he could write to the Philippians, "But I would ye should understand, brethren, that the things which happened unto me have fallen out rather unto the furtherance of the gospel; so that my bonds in Christ are manifest in all the palace, and in all other places" (Phil. 1:12–13). Even when he was in prison he could always say that the Lord stood by him.

"Cast down, but not destroyed." This is tremendous—he was smitten down; the enemy got him down, but the enemy did not destroy or kill him. Actually, in all these phrases Paul is making a play on words which is lost in the translation into English. If I could paraphrase it in English, it would be something like this: "I am struck down, but I'm not struck out." Even at the end of his life Paul could say, ". . . I have *finished* my course . . ." (2 Tim. 4:7, italics mine). Paul seems to be fighting a losing battle. Can't you sense that this man is very weak?

And yet, in his weakness, he is *strong*. If we could have seen this little crippled, weak, sick Jew up against the mighty juggernaut of Roman power, we would have concluded that he was *nothing*. But, my friend, the fact is he brought a message that *withered* the Roman Empire. Even the historian Gibbon said that the Roman Empire could not stand up against the preaching of the gospel of Christ. (May I say that the gospel still continues to topple thrones.) Paul seemed to be so weak, and yet God delivered him again and again. He used miraculous means and He also used natural means. God will never forsake His servants.

You and I live in a day of compromise, a day of expediency, a day when we seem to measure a man by how popular he is or by how many friends he has. The late Dr. Bob Shuler, pastor in downtown Los Angeles, used to say, "I measure a man by the enemies he has." It is important to make the right kind of enemies. Jesus said that if we would love Him and follow Him, the world would hate us. Paul had the right kind of enemies. I am confident that I have the right kind of enemies also.

Always bearing about in the body the dying of the Lord Jesus, that the life also of Jesus might be made manifest in our body [2 Cor. 4:10].

Remember that in 1 Corinthians 15:31 Paul could say that he died daily. In Romans 8:36 he wrote, "As it is written, For thy sake we are killed all the day long; we are accounted as sheep for the slaughter." In 1 Corinthians 4:9 he wrote: "For I think that God hath set forth us the apostles last, as it were appointed to death: for we are made a spectacle unto the world, and to angels, and to men." Christian, do not be afraid to suffer. Jesus said the world would hate us if we were following Him. It is wonderful to take our place with the Lord Jesus Christ in these days.

For we which live are alway delivered unto death for Jesus' sake, that the life also of Jesus might be made manifest in our mortal flesh [2 Cor. 4:11].

We may actually be the strongest at the moment we feel the weakest.

So then death worketh in us, but life in you.

We having the same spirit of faith, according as it is written, I believed, and therefore have I spoken; we also believe, and therefore speak;

Knowing that he which raised up the Lord Jesus shall raise up us also by Jesus, and shall present us with you [2 Cor. 4:12–14].

It is interesting to note here, and this is very important to see, that Paul did not consider death to be the end. He is looking on beyond. Death is merely one of the experiences which he will have. In the next chapter he will speak of the comfort in the ministry of martyrdom for Christ. There is a comfort in laying down your life for Jesus' sake. He is saying here that he is joined to a living Christ. He is dead to the things of the world because he is joined to a living Christ. "He which raised up the Lord Jesus shall raise up us also by Jesus."

For all things are for your sakes, that the abundant grace might through the thanksgiving of many redound to the glory of God.

For which cause we faint not; but though our outward man perish, yet the inward man is renewed day by day [2 Cor. 4:15–16].

This is a wonderful verse. As we grow older, we sort of begin to die out as far as the body is concerned. However, we grow in grace and in the knowledge of Christ. I said to my wife no later than yesterday, "I wish that I were thirty-five years old and knew what I know now." This old body that I have is dying. I can tell it all over. I'm ready to trade it in on a new model. It is beginning to waste away, but the inward man is renewed day by day. I feel closer to the Lord today than I did the day I entered the ministry. I was young then and I had a lot of enthusiasm, but I didn't know very much. What a stumbler I was and how often I failed. I was a real ignoramus then. Now I know a little more; I have grown a little down through the years.

> **For our light affliction, which is but for a moment, worketh for us a far more exceeding and eternal weight of glory;**
>
> **While we look not at the things which are seen, but at the things which are not seen: for the things which are seen are temporal; but the things which are not seen are eternal [2 Cor. 4:17–18].**

Again he makes a contrast. Down here we seem to have a lot of trouble and, my, it does seem to last a long time, doesn't it? It seems so hard. But when we begin to measure it by the weight of glory that is coming someday, it is a *light* affliction compared to that *weight* of glory. Someone has said, "At eventide it shall be light." ". . . we spend our years as a tale that is told" (Ps. 90:9). Our years pass as ". . . a watch in the night" (Ps. 90:4). "For our light affliction, which is but for a moment, worketh for us a far more exceeding and eternal weight of glory." We are not to fix our gaze on the things which are seen. These things that we see around us are all passing away. The things which are not seen are eternal.

I think of the changes that have taken place right here in Southern California. There were a number of very wonderful Christians whom I knew when I came here in 1940. Many of them are gone today. The cities have changed—everything is different. The things which are seen are passing away. The things which are not seen, those are the things of eternal value, and they are beginning to loom larger and larger. "For the things which are seen are temporal; but the things which are not seen are eternal."

My friend, I am looking for that city whose builder and maker is God. I love Pasadena; I love Southern California, but I can truthfully say that I am now looking for another city.

CHAPTER 5

THEME: *God's comfort in the ministry of martyrdom for Christ*

In this section on the comfort of God, we have seen God's comfort in the glorious ministry of Christ (ch. 3). How wonderful that He is an unveiled Christ whom we declare today! Also we have seen God's comfort in the ministry of suffering for Christ (ch. 4), and now we shall see the comfort of God in the ministry of martyrdom for Christ.

> **For we know that if our earthly house of this tabernacle were dissolved, we have a building of God, an house not made with hands, eternal in the heavens [2 Cor. 5:1].**

I want you especially to notice what Paul is saying here. He says, "For we know [not we *hope* or we *expect* or even that we *believe*] that if our earthly house of this tabernacle were dissolved, we have a building of God, an house not made with hands, eternal in the heavens." This is a positive "know." He knows because of the fact that the Spirit of God has made it real to him.

The word for "tabernacle" is skēnē, which means "tent." That is the same word that was used for the wilderness tabernacle of the Old Testament in the Septuagint, a translation of the Old Testament into the Greek. The Old Testament tabernacle, the Mosaic tabernacle, was a skēnē, a tent. It was a flimsy sort of thing.

This verse has always been a big question mark to me. I have never been too dogmatic about the interpretation of it. But I have now come to the conviction that what he is talking about here is *not* a temporary body. For many years I thought that God would have sort of a temporary body for us when we got to heaven. It would be like taking your car to the garage for repair work and having a loaner to drive until it is fixed. I thought that the Lord would give us a temporary body until our new body was given to us. I never liked that idea, but it seemed to be what Paul was saying. Now I don't believe he is referring to a temporary body, because he says it is "eternal in the heavens." He is talking about that new body that we are going to get.

We need to realize that there is an outward man and an inward man. Paul talked about that in the preceding chapter. The outward man perishes, but the inward man is renewed day by day. A great many people misunderstand that. I had a letter from a man who said the Bible is filled with contradictions, and he said, "I can prove there are contradictions. You talk about So-and-So having gone to be with the Lord, and then you talk about the body that is going to be raised and say that the person is going to be raised from the dead down here. Now that is a contradiction." This man has missed the entire point. The body is put in the grave, but the individual, the real person, has gone to be with Christ—if that individual is a believer.

The things that are seen are temporal. Maybe you have seen me and maybe you haven't. When I go to other areas for speaking engagements, some folk drive long distances because they have heard me on the radio and they want to see me. A family in Ohio drove fifty miles just to see how I looked. But actually they didn't see me, they just saw the house, this old tent, I live in. I'll be very frank with you, this old tent is becoming very weak, and it is flapping around. Solomon described old age in Ecclesiastes: "In the day when the keepers of the house shall tremble, and the strong men shall bow themselves, and the grinders cease because they are few, and those that look out of the windows be darkened, and the doors shall be shut in the streets, when the sound of the grinding is low, and he shall rise up at the voice of the bird, and all the daughters of music shall be brought low" (Eccl. 12:3–4). The "keepers of the house" are the legs, and my old knees are beginning to tremble. "The strong men," which are my shoulders, are bowed. My wife tells me to stand up straight, and I tell her I can't stand straight. "Those that look out of the windows" are my eyes— I am wearing trifocals now. "The sound of the grinding is low"—I don't hear as well as I used to hear. This is old age taking place in the outward man. The things that are seen are temporal.

Also, there is an inward man, and the inward man is spiritual. It is difficult for us to understand that. God is a person, but God is not a physical, a material Being. God is a Spirit. "God is a Spirit: and they that worship him must worship him in spirit and in truth."

I hear people say they don't like getting old. My friend, I am enjoying it. I am really enjoying my retirement from a church because I am doing now what I want to do, and it is wonderful to be able to do that. My doctor has told me, "I want you to do what you want to do." When my wife tells me to do something, I say to her, "Look, my doctor tells me to do what I *want* to do, and I don't *want* to do this thing that you want me to do." Sometimes I can get by with that, but not always!

Seriously, it is wonderful to know that every passing year brings me closer to Him. I am going to see Him someday; I am going to see the face of the Lord Jesus, the One who loved me and gave Himself for me. I rejoice in that prospect. To be very frank with you, I don't have as much conflict with the world, the flesh, and the Devil as I used to have. I think they've given up on me. This old house is getting old.

Someone asked President Adams how he felt after he had become an old man. He answered, "I feel fine. This old house that I live in is really getting feeble. The shingles are coming off the top and the foundation seems to be coming out from underneath, but Mr. Adams is just fine, thank you."

My friend, we have a house eternal in the heavens. This body of ours will be sown a natural body, but it will be raised a spiritual body. He is going to give us a new body up yonder.

For in this we groan, earnestly desiring to be clothed upon with our house which is from heaven [2 Cor. 5:2].

I'm groaning in this body. One just can't help but groan. Several years ago I built a study up over my garage, which is right next to the house. I couldn't study in my office at the church; so I transferred my study to this room above the garage. Sometimes, when I start down the steps in the morning, I notice that it isn't as easy as it was some years ago. I used to come bounding down those steps in the morning, but now I groan with every step. My wife tells me, "You ought not to groan like that." I remind her, "It's scriptural to groan. Paul says we groan in this house, and I'm going to groan while I am in this house of mine."

If so be that being clothed we shall not be found naked [2 Cor. 5:3].

This is interesting. One of these days Jesus is going to call His own out of the world. We will be caught up to meet our Lord in the air, and we are going to stand before Him. What will it be like for us? We will be clothed in His righteousness. We will not be found naked.

Not everyone will be clothed in His righteousness when they are raised from the dead. Christ ". . . was delivered for our offences, and was raised again for our justification" (Rom. 4:25)—that is, our righteousness. But some folk have not accepted His righteousness. They have rejected Christ. Therefore, there is a resurrection of the just and of the unjust. Paul mentions this in Acts 24:15, ". . . that there shall be a resurrection of the dead, both of the just and unjust." Jesus said the same thing in John 5:29. "And shall come forth; they that have done good, unto the resurrection of life; and they that have done evil, unto the resurrection of damnation." My friend, you are going to stand in His presence someday. Will you be clothed in the righteousness of Christ? Are you accepted in the Beloved?

This is a good time to mention that the Bible does not teach only one judgment day, but many judgments. (1) There was the judgment which Jesus Christ bore on the Cross. It is because Jesus bore this judgment for us that He could say, "Verily, verily, I say unto you, He that heareth my word, and believeth on him that sent me, hath everlasting life, and shall not come into condemnation [judgment]; but is passed from death unto life" (John 5:24). (2) There is self judgment. We are told in 1 Corinthians 11:31, "For if we would judge ourselves, we should not be judged." (3) Also there is the chastisement of God for the believer. The Lord takes us to His woodshed. "For whom the Lord loveth he chasteneth, and scourgeth every son whom he receiveth" (Heb. 12:6). (4) The works of the believer are to be judged, as we will see later in this chapter. (5) The nation Israel is to be judged. (6) The gentile nations are to be judged. (7) Fallen angels are to be judged. (8) Finally, there is the judgment of the Great White Throne. All the lost ones are brought there. They will appear naked. They will not be clothed in His righteousness. They will be judged according to their works, which is the way they wanted it to be.

> **For we that are in this tabernacle do groan, being burdened: not for that we would be unclothed, but clothed upon, that mortality might be swallowed up of life [2 Cor. 5:4].**

If you feel like groaning, you just groan, my friend. It's scriptural. We are burdened. Yes, we are. That is why we groan in these bodies. It is not that we are worried about being unclothed; we know that we shall be clothed with the righteousness of Christ. If He is our Savior, He is our only hope.

> **Now he that hath wrought us for the selfsame thing is God, who also hath given unto us the earnest of the Spirit [2 Cor. 5:5].**

The earnest of the Spirit implies there is more to follow. He has given us the Holy Spirit down here in these weak bodies with all our feebleness, all our frailty. The Holy Spirit is just the earnest. Earnest money is the down payment. Christ has purchased us, and the Holy Spirit indwelling the believer is the down payment. One of these days we will move out of this old house and we will meet the Lord in the air. How wonderfully this opens up such a vista for us.

> **Therefore we are always confident, knowing that, whilst we are at home in the body, we are absent from the Lord [2 Cor. 5:6].**

We are at home in the body. I like this body of mine. I still have a scar on the side of my temple where I fell against the bed when I was learning to walk. Down through the years I have gotten used to this body of mine, and I feel at home in it. However, as long as I am at home in this body, I am absent from the Lord.

(For we walk by faith, not by sight:) [2 Cor. 5:7].

How could Paul be so sure that when we leave this body we will be present with the Lord? Paul says that we walk by faith. We take God at His Word. I would rather take His Word than anyone else's word. Faith is taking God at His Word. We are living in these bodies, and we are absent from the Lord.

We are confident, I say, and willing rather to be absent from the body, and to be present with the Lord [2 Cor. 5:8].

A better translation would be "at home with the Lord." It contrasts being at home in the body with being at home with the Lord. Remember that the soul does not die. The soul never dies; the soul goes to be with Christ. It is the body that is put to sleep. It is the body that must be changed. Remember that there will be a generation that will not go through death, but their bodies will still need to be changed. "Behold, I shew you a mystery; We shall not all sleep, but we shall all be changed. . . . For this corruptible must put on incorruption, and this mortal must put on immortality" (1 Cor. 15:51, 53). It is the body that goes to sleep and it is the body that is raised. Resurrection does not refer to the soul or the spirit. The English word *resurrection* is the Greek word *anastasis*, which means "a standing up." It is the *body* which will stand up. Knowing these things, we walk by faith.

Wherefore we labour, that, whether present or absent, we may be accepted of him [2 Cor. 5:9].

The Greek word *philotim* that is translated "labour" literally means "to esteem as an honor"—to be ambitious. It is the same Greek word which is translated "study" in 1 Thessalonians 4:11: "And that ye study to be quiet, and to do your own business, and to work with your own hands. . . ." Be ambitious to mind your own business! In the verse before us it is translated "labour"—we should be ambitious, we should labor, in such a way that we will be accepted of Him. This is not ambition to become a great somebody.

We are accepted *in* the Beloved. Paul makes this clear in Ephesians, "Having predestinated us unto the adoption of children by Jesus Christ to himself, according to the good pleasure of his will, to the praise of the glory of his grace, wherein he hath made us accepted in the beloved" (Eph. 1:5–6). Being accepted in Christ is my standing before God. God sees me in Christ, and He is made unto me all that I need: wisdom and righteousness and sanctification and redemption (see 1 Cor. 1:30). He is my perfection. God sees me in Christ, and I am complete in Him. You cannot add anything to completeness. When a person has 100 percent, that person has *all* of it. We who are believers have Christ, and we are accepted *in* the Beloved. Accepted in Christ is the *standing* that all believers have before God.

To be accepted *of* Him is a different thing. This has to do with our *state* and refers to the way we live our lives. Do we live for Christ? Are we ambitious to be accepted of Him? To be ambitious to be accepted of Christ certainly does not mean that we are to crawl over everybody and step on them in order to get to the top. I am afraid we have people in Christian work who are like that because they want to make a name for themselves.

Dr. G. Campbell Morgan tells how he wrestled with this problem. He was a school teacher when he was called as a minister. It was a very solemn moment for him. He felt that the Lord was saying to him, "You have been set apart definitely for the ministry of the Word. Now do you want to be a great preacher, or do you want to be My servant?" The first thought that Dr. Morgan had was, *I want to be a great preacher.* That ought to be a wonderful ambition, but after a while the Lord began to press it in upon him, "Do you want to be a great preacher, or do you want to be My servant?" Finally Dr. Morgan came to it. He saw that he had to make a choice. Finally he said, "O blessed Lord, I would rather be Thy servant than anything else." He was willing to be an obscure preacher. May I say that in my opinion God made G. Campbell Morgan not only His servant but also made him a great preacher. Sometimes we think that our ambition ought to be to do something great for God. God says that He wants us to be His servants. That's all. You and I need to come to the place where we can say, "Lord, just take me and make me and break me and do with me what You will." God gave this word through Jeremiah: "And seekest thou great things for thyself? seek them not . . ." (Jer. 45:5). That's putting it plain enough, isn't it? My friend, are you trying to get great things for yourself? Oh, there are a lot of ambitious laymen and a lot of ambitious Christian workers and a lot of ambitious Christians—but with selfish ambition. Do you really want to be God's servant? If you do, then you can accomplish something for which He will be able to reward you. To be honest with you, I'm beginning to become just a little worried about this. I want to make sure that I am His servant.

1. I am going to have to stand before Him someday and give an account of my service—and so are you. This should motivate us to serve Him acceptably.

For we must all appear before the judgment seat of Christ; that every one may receive the things done in his body, according to that he hath done, whether it be good or bad [2 Cor. 5:10].

This is the judgment seat, literally, the bēma. There is still a bēma in Corinth, and when we were there on tour, we took pictures of the ruins of it. This was the place where the judges of the city would meet the citizens and would judge them for certain things—there was no question of life or death. At the judgment seat of Christ only believers will appear. It is not a judgment of the believer's sins, which Christ fully atoned for on the Cross. The judgment is to see whether you are going to receive a reward or not.

When Paul says, "We must all appear," remember that he is writing to believers. All we believers will be judged, that we may receive the things done in the body. We will be judged on the way we lived the Christian life, how we have lived in these bodies down here. When we go into His presence, we will be finished with these old bodies. The question He will ask is how we *used* these bodies. How did we live down here?

Paul faces this question when he writes to the Philippians. He says in Philippians 1:21, "For to me to live is Christ, and to die is gain." Then he talks of his desire to go to be with Christ but also of his desire to live longer so that he can minister to the Philippians. He wants to stay so that he can preach the gospel of Christ a little longer. I had the same reaction the first time I had surgery for cancer and there was not too much hope for me.

You see, I felt like the little boy years ago in my southland. The preacher asked one night, "How many want to go to heaven?" Everybody put up his hand except that one boy. The preacher looked down at him and said, "Don't you want to go to heaven?" The boy answered, "Sure, I want to go to heaven, but I thought you was gettin' up a load for tonight." Like that boy, I didn't want to go right away when I had the cancer. Paul didn't want to go. He said he wanted to stay in his body and preach a little longer. He wanted Christ to be magnified in his body that he might be accepted of Him and that he might receive a reward.

This is the way I feel. I want to stay in this body and do as much for the Lord as I possibly can. Here is the first motivation for believers: We are all going to appear before the judgment seat of Christ, and we will answer to the Lord for our lives. We are going to give a report to Him. Let me make it very clear that this is not the Great White Throne judgment of Revelation 20:11–15 where only the unsaved will stand. If you are a believer, your name is written in the Book of Life, and you have eternal life. However, you will stand before the bēma, the judgment seat of Christ, to be judged for rewards. You and I will stand before Him. This should motivate us to serve Him acceptably. Then when we come into His presence, He will be able to say, "Well done, thou good and faithful servant."

2. The fear of the Lord urges us to persuade men.

Knowing therefore the terror of the Lord, we persuade men; but we are made manifest unto God; and I trust also are made manifest in your consciences [2 Cor. 5:11].

I think the word *terror* could better be translated "fear." There is a great deal said in the Bible about the fear of the Lord. We are told that the fear of the Lord is the beginning of wisdom (see Prov. 9:10).

One of the tenets of liberalism is that we don't need to be afraid of God. They characterize God as a sweet, indulgent old man whom you can treat most any way. Liberalism teaches the universal fatherhood of God and the universal brotherhood of man, which is one of the most damnable doctrines abroad today. Do you know that the Word of God says: "It is a fearful thing to fall into the hands of the living God" (Heb. 10:31)? Let us not give ersatz bread to the people. Let us not preach a watered-down, sunshiny gospel. Our God is a holy God, a righteous God. It is this holy God who loves you. It is this holy God who wants to save you. But, my friend, if you don't come to God *His* way, you will have to come before Him in judgment. "Knowing therefore the terror [fear] of the Lord, we persuade men." There is many a pulpit from which is never preached a sermon on hell. There are few sermons on punishment, few sermons on judgment. As a result, God's judgment is almost a lost note in Protestantism today. The Lord Jesus said that He had come to seek and to save that which was *lost*. My friend, it is a fearful thing to fall into the hands of the living God. We need to fear the judgment of God. We need to recognize that we are going to be held accountable to Him.

For we commend not ourselves again unto you, but give you occasion to glory on our behalf, that ye may have somewhat to answer them which glory in appearance, and not in heart [2 Cor. 5:12].

In other words, if you are declaring the full counsel of God, you can do it in a loving manner. You don't have to bring down thunder and lightning. However, we need to recognize and we need to state very clearly that men are lost. If we do say that, we are not commending ourselves; that is, we are not trying to become popular. I am always afraid of the soft-soap type of thing we hear today. There is so much today that goes the way of psychology, how to become a well-adjusted human being. May I say to you that if you are without Christ, it is not a psychological adjustment that you need. You are a hell-doomed sinner, and you are on the way to hell. What you need is Christ!

It may not make me popular to say this to you, but it is the Word of God. We don't commend ourselves to you. We don't want you to glory in us. The important thing for us to do is to declare the whole counsel of God. Our motivation to get out the Word of God is a recognition of God's judgment. That is the thing that would arouse many a sleepy church member today.

Missionaries come and tell about the needs out yonder. May I say that there is a real need in this land of ours. The United States is one of the greatest mission fields today. People in our land are on the way to hell. You rub shoulders with them every day.

> **For whether we be beside ourselves, it is to God: or whether we be sober, it is for your cause [2 Cor. 5:13].**

Paul says that the people may think he is crazy. That is all right. He is doing this for God. Or some people may think he is sober—well, it is for their sakes that he is sober.

3. The love of Christ constrains us.

> **For the love of Christ constraineth us; because we thus judge, that if one died for all, then were all dead:**
>
> **And that he died for all, that they which live should not henceforth live unto themselves, but unto him which died for them, and rose again [2 Cor. 5:14–15].**

"Constraineth us" is a phrase that has been misunderstood. The thought has been that the love of Christ restricts us or straps us down. That is not the meaning of the word that Paul is using here. He says it is the love of Christ that is pushing us out. It is the love of Christ that is motivating us. It is the love of Christ that causes us to give out the Word of God. The love of Christ constrains us.

"Because we thus judge, that if one died for all, then were all dead." It was this that sent Paul out to the ends of the earth with the message of the gospel.

"Because we thus judge, that if one died for all, then were all dead." Mankind is under the sentence of death. When Adam was yonder in the Garden of Eden, he was our federal head; he was the head of that old creation. That old creation was on trial in Adam. God told him, ". . . Of every tree of the garden thou mayest freely eat: But of the tree of the knowledge of good and evil, thou shalt not eat of it: for in the day that thou eatest thereof thou shalt surely die" (Gen. 2:16–17). Adam deliberately disobeyed God. He came under the sentence of death, and when he did that, he took the entire human race down with him, for all were represented in him. You and I have been born into a family of death. All mankind now is under the sentence of death.

Someone has said, "The very moment that gives you life begins to take it away from you." When David wrote, "Yea, though I walk through the valley of the shadow of death . . ." (Ps. 23:4), he was not referring to the end of life; he was saying that all of life is like walking down through the great canyon of death, which gets darker and narrower until, finally, we must go through that doorway of death.

Dr. Ironside used to illustrate this in an unusual way, and I'll give you my version of his very wonderful illustration. Behind my home is a lovely range of mountains called the San Gabriels. Mount Wilson is in this range, and on top of Mount Wilson is the Hale observatory. Now let's think of Mount Wilson as representing Paradise, the place where God put man when He first created him. Adam had everything that was good for him, but there was one thing that God told him he was not to do. Adam was a sinless man and he faced a choice. God had asked him not to do one thing, and that was the very thing which Adam did. He fell. We call it the fall of Adam. He came tumbling down off that high mountain and landed way down in the valley where we are today. After he had fallen down into the valley he began to bring into this world a race of people. They don't come into this world way up yonder where Adam had been on the mountaintop, on the plane where he had been when he was innocent, but down in the valley, the place to which Adam fell.

The Lord Jesus Christ came to this world all the way from heaven. He was the absolutely sinless One. He was holy, harmless, undefiled, separate from sinners. He came down here to save sinners. He came down from heaven, but He didn't go to the mountaintop. There are no people there—He couldn't find any man on that plane of holiness. They are all in the valley. They are all dead in trespasses and sins. So what did He do? He came down into the valley. He came down into the place of death where all men are. "And that he died for all." Because men were dead, He went down into death, and now He brings believers up with Him in resurrection life. Does He take them back up to the mountaintop where Adam had been? No, He takes them with Him into the heavenlies. We who believe in the Lord Jesus Christ are now seated in the heavenlies. He has ". . . raised us up together, and made us sit together in heavenly places in Christ Jesus" (Eph. 2:6).

"If one died for all, then were all dead." He took our place. And those who believe on Him are risen with Him. They are not risen so they can be put back on the mountaintop and come tumbling down again. No, He takes them all the way up to the heavenlies. Christ took our place. And if we are going to live, it is going to be by faith in Him—that those through faith "should not henceforth live unto themselves, but unto him which died for them, and rose again." Christ died, not only that we should be delivered from death and judgment, but also that we should be brought up from our state of death into newness of life. Now our lives should be devoted to Him that we should live henceforth to the glory of God.

For the child of God this puts a whole new interpretation on the human family.

> **Wherefore henceforth know we no man after the flesh: yea, though we have known Christ after the flesh, yet now henceforth know we him no more [2 Cor. 5:16].**

Now we do not know men "after the flesh." Now we see men through different eyes from those we used when we belonged to the world. Out in the world there are only lost men. I know a Ph.D. who teaches at Cal Tech in Pasadena. He is a brilliant fellow, but he is a lost man because he is not in Christ. I know a man from the gutter; he is also a lost man because he is not in Christ. "Henceforth know we no man after the flesh." That is to say, we do not evaluate men according to their racial background or their social background or their color. We know that according to the old nature they are all lost in sin. But Christ died for all of them. Christ died for the Ph.D. and He died for the man in the gutter. He died for all.

James writes about this in the second chapter of his epistle. He says it is wrong to give the honored place to a rich man who comes into your midst with a ring on his finger and with fine clothing on his back while you give the poor fellow a place to stand in the back. Why is that wrong? Because as the children of God we are to look upon the whole human family as sinners for whom Christ died. Even the line between Jew and Gentile has been erased. All in the human family are sinners before God. The only solution for all is the gospel of Jesus Christ. We do not recognize any man after the flesh. All are on the same level.

"Though we have known Christ after the flesh, yet now henceforth know we him no more." I believe that Paul did know Christ after the flesh. I think that he was present at the crucifixion of Christ. I can't imagine that brilliant young Pharisee not being present at the Crucifixion in Jerusalem.

Jesus Christ walked on this earth over nineteen hundred years ago. He was born in Bethlehem, raised in Nazareth, walked in Galilee, began His ministry in Cana of Galilee, went to Jerusalem, died on a cross there, was buried outside the city in Joseph's tomb, rose again the third day, appeared to those who were His own, and ascended back into heaven. We don't know Him anymore as the Man of Galilee, friend. There is no man of Galilee today.

At Christmastime there are a great many people who make a trek to Bethlehem. The place is crowded. What are they looking for? Are they looking for the Babe? He isn't there! Jerusalem is crowded with tourists at Eastertime. Our risen Lord isn't there. You see, we don't know Him after the flesh anymore.

Right now, at this very moment, He is up yonder at God's right hand. He is the glorified Christ. "Though we have known Christ after the flesh," now we don't know Him that way anymore. We are not identified with the One who walked on this earth over nineteen hundred years ago; we are identified with Him who is in glory. That is why it says that we have died with Him and have risen with Him and are now in Christ Jesus in the heavenlies.

> **Therefore if any man be in Christ, he is a new creature: old things are passed away; behold, all things are become new [2 Cor. 5:17].**

Here we have a tremendous statement. Allow me to change the word *creature* to the word *creation*. "If any man be in Christ, he is a new creation." We hear this verse often at testimony meetings. People will quote this verse and tell about their conversion. They say they no longer indulge in certain bad habits that they had before their conversion, and they consider this change in their habits to be a fulfillment of this verse.

If you and I are a new creation in Christ Jesus, what are the old things that have passed away? Remember that we have talked about all mankind living at the bottom of the hill where all of us are sinners. Now that we have trusted Christ, those old relationships have passed away. We are no longer identified with Adam. We are no longer identified with the world system. We are now identified with Christ. We have been baptized into the body of believers and we belong to Him. The old things have passed away, and the new thing is this new relationship to the Lord Jesus Christ. We are now in a relationship with the glorified Christ.

Let's be very practical about this. You may ask, "I know that is a wonderful verse, but how may I know absolutely that I am a new creation in Christ?" Listen to what the Lord Jesus said: "Verily, verily, I say unto you, He that heareth my word, and believeth on him that sent me, hath everlasting life, and shall not come into condemnation; but is passed from death unto life" (John 5:24). Have you believed in the Lord Jesus Christ? Do you trust Him? If you do, He assures you that you have eternal life and will not come into judgment; you have passed from death unto life. This makes you a new creation, no longer subject to judgment and death. You have passed into life.

Do not try to base your confidence on experience. You are a new creation because Jesus says so. The basis is the Word of God. You no longer belong to the old creation that fell in Adam. The new creation stands in Christ Jesus, and you are *in Him* if you are putting your trust in Him. You and I stand in the place of danger and temptation; we may fail in many, many ways, but the wonderful truth is that the Lord Jesus Christ has redeemed us and we are a new creation in Him.

Now Paul is going on to talk about that.

> **And all things are of God, who hath reconciled us to himself by Jesus Christ, and hath given to us the ministry of reconciliation [2 Cor. 5:18].**

The ministry of reconciliation is actually God's call to lost men everywhere to come to Him with all their sins, all their burdens, all their problems, all their difficulties, and to be reconciled to God. I want to spend some time here to look at this matter of reconciliation. The word is used twice in this verse, twice in the next verse, and once in the following verse. Verse 21 doesn't have the word in it, but it sums it all up. This is a most important subject, and we are in a very important section here.

First let me state that reconciliation is not the same as salvation. Reconciliation goes a step further. It is more than having our sins forgiven and divine justice being satisfied. Reconciliation involves a changed relationship—completely changed. It means to change something inside out and upside down and right side up. "If any man be in Christ he is a new creation."

Notice that there is the Godward side of reconciliation. He is the One who did the reconciling. "God, who hath reconciled us to himself by Jesus Christ." It is repeated in the next verse.

> **To wit, that God was in Christ, reconciling the world unto himself, not imputing their trespasses unto them; and hath committed unto us the word of reconciliation [2 Cor. 5:19].**

Reconciliation is the ministry of changing completely. But who is changing completely? God is never changing—He is the same yesterday, today, and forever. It says that God has reconciled *us* to Himself. "God was in Christ, reconciling the *world* unto himself." It is the world that has been reconciled. God has reconciled the world. As we look at the world, we can see that it is going on its sinful way. "We have turned everyone to his own way" (see Isa. 53:6). But it is through Christ that the world is reconciled to God, through the *death* of Christ. This marvelous ministry of reconciliation is the work that Christ has done.

Let me call in another passage of Scripture concerning this. "And, having made peace through the blood of his cross, by him to reconcile all things unto himself; by him, I say, whether they be things in earth, or things in heaven. And you, that were sometime alienated and enemies in your mind by wicked works, yet now hath he reconciled in the body of his flesh through death, to present you holy and unblameable and unreproveable in his sight" (Col. 1:20–22). Compare this with Philippians 2:10 in which it says that at the name of Jesus every knee will bow, of things in heaven, and things in earth, and things under the earth—"*under* the earth" refers to hell. I want you to notice in the passage in Colossians, when it is speaking of reconciliation, only *heaven* and *earth* are mentioned. Hell is not reconciled to God. Although every being in hell will bow to Him, only those in heaven and earth are reconciled. In what way are they reconciled? "And you, that were sometime alienated and enemies in your mind by wicked works, yet now hath he reconciled in the body of his flesh through death, to present you holy and unblameable and unreproveable in his sight" (Col. 1:21–22). The death of Christ is what reconciled the world to God.

Notice that *God* is not reconciled—He has not changed. But the world has been put in a different position. Why? Because Christ died. You see, when Adam sinned back there in the Garden of Eden, a holy God couldn't reach down and save him. God had to do something about his sin. God had to judge man. "The soul that sinneth, it shall die . . ." (Ezek. 18:20). God had told Adam, ". . . for in the day that thou eatest thereof thou shalt surely die" (Gen. 2:17). Adam did die spiritually on that very day, and nine hundred years later he also died physically. When he died spiritually, he became alienated and separated from God; and he had no capacity for God. That is the condition of the world, and God had to judge that.

Now that Christ has died, the position of the world has been changed. Today God has His arms outstretched to a lost world. He says to a lost world, "You can come to Me." The worst sinner in the world can come to Him. Today it doesn't make any difference who you are, you can come to Him. Because Christ died, a holy God no longer deals with us in judgment, but now He reaches down to save all those who will come to Him. Jesus Christ bore all that judgment on Himself so that now the world is reconciled to God. You don't have to do anything to win God over. God is not waiting around the corner to hit you over the head with a billy club. God is not angry with you. God does not hate you. God *loves* you. Christ did not come to charge man's sins against him but to pay man's debt.

The woman taken in adultery is an illustration of this (see John 8:1–11). The Lord Jesus said to that crowd of hypocritical religious leaders, ". . . He that is without sin among you, let him first cast a stone at her." Then Jesus wrote something in the sand, wrote something on the earth. It is interesting that in Jeremiah 17:13 it says, ". . . they that depart from me shall be written in the earth, because they have forsaken the LORD, the fountain of living waters."

It tells us that they left—beginning with the old Pharisees and then down to the younger ones. The older ones had more sense than the young fellows who hung around a little longer. I think probably one of the old fellows had had an affair with a woman over in Corinth. He thought nobody knew about it, but of course the Lord knew all about it. Perhaps Jesus just wrote down the name of that girl, and when the old Pharisee looked down and saw that name written on the ground, he said, "I just remembered I have another engagement," and he tore out of there in a hurry. Before long they were all gone except one— only Jesus Christ was left. The only One who could have thrown a stone at her did not throw a stone. He asked, "Woman, where are those thine accusers? hath no man condemned thee? She said, No man, Lord. And Jesus said unto her, Neither do I condemn thee: go, and sin no more" (John 8:10–11). "God was in Christ, reconciling the world unto himself, not imputing their trespasses unto them." Jesus was not shutting His eyes to her sin, but for all that sin He was going to the Cross. The condemnation was to fall on Him, and because she trusted Him, He could send her away uncondemned.

> **Now then we are ambassadors for Christ, as though God did beseech you by us: we pray you in Christ's stead, be ye reconciled to God [2 Cor. 5:20].**

Who is an ambassador? Webster says an ambassador is a minister of the highest rank accredited to a foreign government or sovereign as the official representative of his own government or sovereign. "Now then we are ambassadors for Christ." We are in a foreign land—Peter says that we are pilgrims and strangers down here. Paul says, "For our conversation [citizenship] is in heaven; from whence also we look for the Saviour, the Lord Jesus Christ" (Phil. 3:20). Since our citizenship is in heaven, we are ambassadors down here.

When one government sends an ambassador to another government, it means they are on friendly relations. God is still friendly with this world. He has sent us as His ambassadors. One day He will call His ambassadors home. Then judgment will begin.

When man sinned, God in His holiness had to turn away from the world. But God loved man, so He sent His own Son to die on the Cross. Now God can hold out His arms to the world and say, "You can come." We are His ambassadors. As His ambassadors, we are to tell folk, "God will save you!" All God is asking any man to do is to come to Him. God will not try to get even with you. He doesn't want to punish you. He doesn't want to lay a hand on you. He invites all people everywhere to come to Him.

This is a great day. We have the privilege of saying to you, "Be ye reconciled to God." All He asks you to do is to turn to Him. How can He do this? It is because Christ bore it all for us.

> On Him almighty vengeance fell
> That would have sunk a world to hell,
> He bore it for a chosen race,
> And thus becomes our hiding place.

God is reconciled. You don't need to do one thing to win Him over. You don't have to shed tears to soften the heart of God. He loves you. He wants to save you. Why?

> **For he hath made him to be sin for us, who knew no sin; that we might be made the righteousness of God in him [2 Cor. 5:21].**

Jesus Christ took my place down here. He, who knew no sin, came that we might be made the righteousness of God in Him. He has given me His place, clothed in His righteousness, He took my hell down here so that I might have His heaven up yonder. He did that for me.

Christian friend, have you been able to get out this wonderful Word to anyone else? Whoever you are, wherever you are, however you are, what are you doing today to get this Word of reconciliation out to a lost world? God is reconciled. He is the same yesterday, today, and forever. He feels toward you just as He did the day Christ died on the Cross for you and for all mankind. This is what the world needs to hear from you. The world is reconciled to Him, but they will have to turn around and by faith come to Him. Let's get this word out, my friend.

CHAPTER 6

THEME: God's comfort in all circumstances of the ministry of Christ

We find set before us here the requirements of a good minister of Jesus Christ. None of us can read this without saying again, "Who is sufficient for these things?" None of us could meet these high standards. But I want you to notice that we are still in the section of God's comfort. Here we see God's comfort in all circumstances of the ministry of Christ.

TRYING EXPERIENCES OF THE MINISTRY

We then, as workers together with him, beseech you also that ye receive not the grace of God in vain [2 Cor. 6:1].

You will notice in your Bible that "with him" is in italics, which means that these two words have been supplied by the translators. It should be "We then, as workers together."

There is a line that needs to be rubbed out, and that is the line between the clergy and laity. There are certain ones who have been given the gift of teaching. If I have any gift, it would have to be that one, because if I can't claim that one, I don't have any at all. There are those who are gifted to teach, those who are gifted to be missionaries. We would term them the clergy. But God gives a gift to each member of the body of Christ. There ought not to be the distinction between the pulpit and the pew that we make today. We are all workers together. If you are one who sits in the pew, may I say that you are as responsible to give out the word of God as I am. I have been given the gift of teaching. You may be a bank president or the president of a large corporation, a truck driver, a housewife, but you are responsible today to get out the Word of God. God has given to the church certain men who will teach, certain men who will act as pastors, certain men who have gifts that are used for the work of the ministry, which is the equipping of the believers to serve.

Again let me read the comment of Dr. Earl Radmacher, who is currently president of the Western Conservative Baptist Seminary: "Shepherds do not produce sheep. Sheep produce sheep." You see, a great many people think it is the business of the evangelist and the preacher to win people for Christ. May I say to you that it is *your* business. God has given teachers and preachers and evangelists and missionaries to fill out and prepare the body of believers so that those who are sitting in the pews might be equipped for their ministry of going out to witness for Christ. The shepherd doesn't produce the sheep. He feeds the sheep and he watches over the sheep. He shepherds the sheep, but he doesn't produce sheep. He can't. The sheep produce sheep.

Today the whole work of the church is bogged down because the sheep are not out witnessing. I want to raise the question again, and I know I am being very personal about it, what are *you* doing today to get the Word of God out to others? You can do something that I cannot do and that no preacher in the country can do. There are some people who have confidence in you. They will listen to you but they won't listen to a preacher—unless you encourage them to listen. I know a very fine businessman who has a speech impediment and doesn't feel he can speak very well to people. He takes tapes from our program and circulates them everywhere. He knocks on the door of one of his workers or associates, takes along a tape and a tape recorder, and invites them to listen to the tape with him. There is an example of witnessing. We are workers together.

Then Paul says, "We . . . beseech you also that ye receive not the grace of God in vain." How can one receive the grace of God in vain? God has been showering His goodness and mercy on us. To receive His great goodness and to rejoice in the salvation of the grace of God and yet to live carnal, worldly lives is what it means to receive the grace of God in vain. Let me ask you this question: What response are we making today to the love of God's heart?

(For he saith, I have heard thee in a time accepted, and in the day of salvation have I succoured thee: behold, now is the accepted time; behold, now is the day of salvation.) [2 Cor. 6:2].

"Have I succoured thee" means I have helped you.

A great many people say, "Well, I won't accept Christ now. I will do it some other time." They postpone it. Some people want to wait until a certain evangelist comes to town or until they can attend a great meeting. Now I don't know who you are or where you are right now, but if you are not saved, "now is the accepted time." Look at your clock. Whatever time it is right *now* is the time for you. Somebody will ask, "Can't I accept Him tomorrow?" Probably, but you have no promise of a tomorrow. The important thing is that God says the time is right now.

Giving no offence in any thing, that the ministry be not blamed [2 Cor. 6:3].

We need to be very careful about personal behavior. We are to give no offense in anything. An offense here doesn't mean hurting people's feelings. I don't think anyone can serve in the church today without hurting the feelings of someone. Some folk are there for no other purpose than to get their feelings hurt. You have heard the old saying about carrying your feelings on your sleeve. Well, a lot of the saints do just that. Dr. Harry Ironside put it something like this: If you don't shake hands with them, they feel you intended to slight them. If you do shake hands with them, you hurt their arthritis. If you stop to speak with them, you are interrupting them. But if you do not, you are a little snooty. If you write them a letter, they know you are after their money. If you do not write, then you are neglecting them. If you stop to visit them you hinder them from their work and bother them, but if you do not visit them, it shows you have no interest in them.

My wife and I got up early one morning and drove two hundred miles before breakfast. We were really hungry and we stopped in a dumpy little place where they served a good Texas breakfast with grits and hot biscuits. When I went to pay the bill, I noticed a sign up by the cash register. "We can't please everybody but we try." That may be a familiar sign to you, but it was new to me that morning and it made my day.

"Giving no offence" means that you are so to live that no one can point to you and say, "Because of that man's life I have no confidence in the salvation he professes."

Now Paul lists things that should characterize the ministry. They are quite interesting.

But in all things approving ourselves as the ministers of God, in much patience, in afflictions, in necessities, in distresses [2 Cor. 6:4].

"In much patience." That is number one on the list. Believe me, I am bowled over by this very first one. I'll be very frank to admit to you that patience is something I have always lacked. My wife and my best friends say this to me: "Vernon McGee, if you ever preach a sermon on patience and I am there, I'm going to walk out because I don't think you are the fellow to speak on patience." So do you know what? I'm not going to speak about patience now. I just want you to notice it is number one on the list.

"In afflictions." This is something that a great many men in the ministry today must still bear.

"In necessities." Folk who came through the depression or who were born in a poor home understand this. When I was a boy, I saw the time that there was not a one dollar bill in my home. We would have gone hungry had it not been for the fact that the grocer would sell us groceries on credit. There was many a time I had nothing in the world for supper, the evening meal, but just a glass of sweet milk with crumbled, cold biscuits in it. And do you want to know something? I still think that is delicious. It is better than a lot of French pastry I have eaten.

Dr. Harry Ironside tells about the time he as a young preacher preached in a place for three days and didn't have a thing to eat during those three days. He was preaching to a group of people who thought he was living by faith, and they surely did let him do it. No money was given him for food. On the fourth morning he was debating whether to stay in bed for breakfast or to get up and tighten up his belt another notch when he noticed a letter being slipped under the door. He got up and opened it and all it said was, "Enclosed is an expression of Christian fellowship," and there was a ten dollar bill in it. That morning he went out and had the best breakfast he had ever had in his life.

"In afflictions, in necessities, in distresses." There are a great many folk living today who know what these are. The younger generation doesn't know. That is what has made the generation gap. I try to tell my daughter about the Depression. She answers me, "Dad, I don't even know what you are talking about." And she doesn't know.

In stripes, in imprisonments, in tumults, in labours, in watchings, in fastings [2 Cor. 6:5].

"In stripes." I have a notion that very few of us know what physical stripes are such as Paul experienced. "Stripes" consisted of forty blows with a rod. However, we have been cut across the face many times by some insulting remark made by some pious saint in a very pious voice. There used to be a dear lady in my congregation who had a very sharp tongue. She would go out of the evening service and would say to me, "Pastor, you had a wonderful sermon this morning"—implying that I could preach a good sermon in the morning but that the evening sermon was not good. That is a way some folk hit a minister across the face.

Paul lists other things that he experienced in his ministry (which few men in my day have had to pass through): Imprisonments, tumults, labors, watchings, fastings—all were familiar to Paul.

Now he goes on to give another set of identifications of the ministry.

By pureness, by knowledge, by longsuffering, by kindness, by the Holy Ghost, by love unfeigned,

By the word of truth, by the power of God, by the armour of righteousness on the right hand and on the left [2 Cor. 6:6–7].

"By pureness." Believe me, it is important that a minister be pure in his life. Lack of pureness is one thing that hits and hurts the ministry today. It is always tragic when a minister turns up as a bad egg and is found guilty of immorality and impurity. Pureness is important—and it is important to God. "By knowledge." I do not think that knowledge refers only to a knowledge of the Word of God. A minister of the Word should know a great many things, and he should keep himself abreast of the times in which he lives. "By longsuffering." Here that comes up again. Longsuffering is patience in a different suit of clothes. "By kindness." Oh, how folk long to have a pastor who has tender, kindly interest in them! "By the Holy Ghost." God have mercy on any preacher who tries to preach without the Spirit of God leading and guiding. I am more concerned about that than any other thing. I was pastor in downtown Los Angeles for twenty-one years, and I had followed many great men. I often thought about Dr. R. A. Torrey, the great evangelist of the past, who had been the first pastor of the church. When I would go out to preach, the last thing I would say was, "O Lord, help me to preach in the power of the Holy Spirit!" Vernon McGee in himself is not very much in comparison to those men who went before him. An effective ministry can only be by the Holy Ghost. "By love unfeigned." Genuine love is so desperately needed today. We do not need pious pretenders quoting pious platitudes. We do not need phony professors of faith who tell you how much they love you and then put a knife in your back. We need real, genuine love. We need the love that the Spirit of God puts into hearts. "By the word of truth." The "word of truth" means that a preacher should know his Bible. He should preach "by the power of God," which is possible only as a pastor spends time alone with God before he steps into the pulpit. "By the armour of righteousness on the right hand and on the left" is right living in all areas.

Next Paul gives us a set of nine paradoxes which should characterize a man of God.

By honour and dishonour, by evil report and good report: as deceivers, and yet true;

As unknown, and yet well known; as dying, and, behold, we live; as chastened, and not killed;

As sorrowful, yet alway rejoicing; as poor, yet making many rich; as having nothing, and yet possessing all things [2 Cor. 6:8–10].

"By honour and dishonour." Some may approve and some may disapprove. This gives a well-balanced ministry. "By evil report and good report." Although some folk will say ugly things about us, we continue to serve the Lord. Shakespeare has one of his characters say, "They praise me and make an ass of me; now my foes tell me plainly I am an ass: so that by my foes, sir, I profit in the knowledge of myself, and by my friends I am abused." Flattery harms us more than criticism! "As deceivers, and yet true"—we are called deceivers, yet we are giving out the true Word of God. "As unknown, and yet well known." A minister of God may not be well known to the world, but he is known to God. "As dying, and, behold, we live"—Paul had taken the place of death, yet he had had new life in Christ. "Chastened, and not killed." He often experienced persecution, beatings, whippings, stonings, and yet he lived on. "Sorrowful, yet alway rejoicing." Sorrow was for the sins of the people and their rejection of the gospel, yet he was rejoicing in Christ. "As poor, yet making many rich." Whenever you find a minister who is rich, watch out. Folk are not supposed to get rich in the ministry. "Having nothing, and yet possessing all things." You recall that Paul had said in his first letter to the Corinthians that all things were theirs. This includes things in the world, life, death, present or future. ". . . All are yours; and ye are Christ's; and Christ is God's" (1 Cor. 3:22–23)—oh, how rich we are! And yet we are poor.

Paul has given us three sets of things which characterize the ministry. You will notice that the first set pertains to things which are physical, the second to things which are mental, and the third to things which are spiritual. All are important.

PERSONAL APPEAL OF PAUL

Paul just seems to cry out here. Oh, how ye yearned for those converts of his in Corinth. They are little baby Christians, babes in Christ, carnal Christians, but his heart went out to them. It seems his heart almost breaks in this chapter and the next one.

> O ye Corinthians, our mouth is open unto you, our heart is enlarged.
>
> Ye are not straitened in us, but ye are straitened in your own bowels.
>
> Now for a recompence in the same, (I speak as unto my children,) be ye also enlarged [2 Cor. 6:11–13].

Paul is opening up his great heart of love, and he stirs up the hearts of those who love him. The interesting thing is that he apparently also stirred up the hearts of those who hated God and His Word and who tried to work injury upon those who loved Him and loved the Scripture. We find that was true in the early history of the church, and it is true today. If you stand for God, you will find that it will really cost you something.

We come now to an important passage of Scripture. It is a section which has been often abused and misinterpreted. Some folk try to make it hard as nails, unyielding and unloving. Yet what Paul is saying here is coming from the tender heart of a man whose heart was almost breaking because of his great concern for the Corinthian believers.

> Be ye not unequally yoked together with unbelievers: for what fellowship hath righteousness with unrighteousness? and what communion hath light with darkness? [2 Cor. 6:14].

Paul here makes an appeal to the Corinthian believers to make a clean break with idolatry. They are to make a break from the sins of the flesh. They are to be separated from the worldliness that is in the world. Today we use the term "separated believers." There are many folk who consider themselves to be "separated believers" who are actually as worldly as can be.

Back in the Old Testament under the Mosaic Law God gave a law to His people who were largely engaged in agriculture. He said that they were not to yoke together an ox and an ass. That would be yoking together unequal animals.

One was a clean animal and the other was an unclean animal. Here God is speaking to believers, and He says that the believer should not be yoked together with an unbeliever. How are people yoked together? Well, they are yoked together in any form of real union such as a business enterprise, a partnership, a marriage, a long-term enterprise.

Certainly marriage is the yoking together of two people. An unbeliever and a believer should not marry. A clean animal and an unclean animal should not be yoked together to plow. A child of God and a child of the Devil cannot be yoked together and pull together in their life goals.

Another example of such a relationship is identification with an institution. If a man is a professor in a seminary and he is conservative and holds the great truths of the Bible, but the seminary has gone liberal, such a man should get out of that seminary, because he is drawing a salary there and he is identified with their work and their organization. He is associated with it in a very tangible, real way. He is unequally yoked with unbelievers.

Suppose, however, that an evangelist comes to town and holds services for one or two weeks. Although he uses certain methods that you would not condone, he is preaching Christ and God is blessing his ministry, are you to join with him?

When I was a pastor in Nashville, Tennessee, an evangelist came to town and, without saying a word to any of us who were conservative men, put his tent right across from my church and the Baptist church in that end of the city. Then he came over to solicit our help. I was somewhat reluctant because of the ethics of the man. He was really a sort of screwball in many ways. He would conduct the most informal services. He would stop in the middle of his sermon because he had forgotten to make an announcement or had forgotten to take up an offering. The Baptist pastor and I were good friends and both conservative, so we talked it over. We didn't like all the methods of the evangelist, but we decided that we would support him. He was there for a couple of weeks and people were saved through his ministry. I would never have joined with him in any sort of permanent commitment because of his methods, but I gave him my support for the time he was there. We were by no means yoked together.

Notice how Paul did it. Paul would first go to the synagogue when he entered into a new city. Can you imagine a place where there would be more opposition to Jesus Christ than in the synagogue? Yet that is where Paul began. I am not condemning him for it because God led him to do it that way. Now if Paul had *joined* himself to one of those synagogues and had become the rabbi in one of them and had stayed there, then that could have been considered a yoke.

You see, Paul is talking about being yoked together in a permanent arrangement like marriage or a business partnership or a professorship in a school or membership in a church. This verse has no reference to my support of an evangelistic crusade. There are many men who do not carry on their ministries the way I do mine—and some of them are so much more successful than I am, that maybe they are right and I am wrong. Of course, I feel that I am right and I intend to go along as I am now. But this won't keep me from having fellowship with men who do things a little differently as long as they are preaching the same gospel that I preach and they believe the Bible is the Word of God. Paul is talking about yoking ourselves with *unbelievers*, as he makes clear in the next verse.

And what concord hath Christ with Belial? or what part hath he that believeth with an infidel? [2 Cor. 6:15].

Well, I certainly don't have any part with them. I am not joining with them permanently in anything, and I trust you are not. Let's not confuse this with our relationship with other believers who do things in a different way from what we do them.

And what agreement hath the temple of God with idols? for ye are the temple of the living God; as God hath said, I will dwell in them, and walk in them; and I will be their God, and they shall be my people [2 Cor. 6:16].

Now Paul specifically mentions idolatry. The temple of God has no agreement with idols. Where is the temple of God? Today the temple of God is the human body of each and every believer. We are the temples of the Holy Spirit. The one in whom God dwells cannot be in agreement with idols.

Wherefore come out from among them, and be ye separate, saith the Lord, and touch not the unclean thing; and I will receive you,

And will be a Father unto you, and ye shall be my sons and daughters, saith the Lord Almighty [2 Cor. 6:17–18].

Paul is appealing to the Christian for separation and for cleansing. He is not to be in agreement with idolatry. He is to be separate from worldliness and from the spirit of worldliness which can creep even into the churches and into the lives of believers. The believer should not even touch the unclean thing.

Back in the Book of Joshua we learned how Joshua and the Israelites took the fortified city of Jericho by faith. However, Achan took the "accursed thing." Israel had touched what God had declared to be unclean. Then they went up to the little city of Ai with great confidence because they were sure of an easy victory, but Joshua and Israel were overcome and defeated at Ai. God asks for a separation from worldliness and from the unclean thing.

There are a great many Christians who consider themselves separated. They wouldn't think of doing this or of doing that. Yet they gossip and have the meanest tongues, never realizing that that very thing is worldly and unclean. Or they go in for the latest in dress or for gluttony and yet consider themselves to be separate from worldliness. I don't mean to sit in judgment—and we ought not to sit in judgment on each other—yet I feel I must point out these things because we need to be very, very careful. It is very easy to talk about the things of God, to claim the Lord Jesus Christ as Savior, to say we love Him, to consider ourselves separated unto Him, and still not in reality be separate from the world and separated unto Him.

When I made my decision to enter the ministry, the vice-president of the bank where I worked called me into his office. He was a godless man—he could swear as I've never heard anyone swear. I think it rather moved him when I announced that I was giving up my job to study for the ministry. He called me over to his desk and said, "Vernon, I want to tell you a story." This is what he told me: During World War I he was working in another bank and with him worked a man as godless and worldly as could be. However, this man was the soloist in a church. One day the man who was now the vice-president went to church, and there he heard his co-worker sing a solo, "Jesus Satisfies." A dear lady said to him afterwards, "Wasn't that a marvelous solo? It sounds like it came out of heaven!" Since he knew this man at work, he knew that Jesus did not satisfy him. One day this same woman came into the bank to do some business, and the teller who had been the soloist was attempting to get a balance sheet balanced, but it was off, and he began to rip out oaths and curses. The lady was really shocked at this and asked my friend, "Who is that man?" He answered, "That is the voice you heard the other Sunday and thought it came right out of heaven." The vice-president of the bank was a skeptic and a rascal because he had seen a professing Christian singing, "Jesus Satisfies," when he knew Jesus did not satisfy that man. He knew that man was immoral, a drinker, and a man of vile language. He knew a Christian should not be like that, and it made him a cynical individual. He reached over and touched me on the knee and said to me, "Vernon, don't be a preacher unless you mean it." I have never forgotten that.

God says, "Come out from among them, and be ye separate, . . . and touch not the unclean thing." Don't be a Christian unless you mean it. Don't say that Jesus satisfies you if He is not really satisfying you. This is what Paul is talking about.

Then there is this glorious promise: "And I will receive you, and will be a Father unto you, and ye shall be my sons and daughters, saith the Lord Almighty." You will be the kind of son or daughter who brings honor to the Father.

A man told me about his boy going away to college. The boy had become alienated from his dad. He was still the man's son, but the father said to me, "I can't deal with him as I would like to as a father. I simply can't talk to him the way I'd like to as a father." This is what God is saying here.

If you are a believer in Jesus Christ, God is always your Father. Don't forget that. What God is saying here is that He would like to act like a Father to you. He would like to treat you as a son. If you are going off into worldliness, if you don't mean what you say, if you are hypocritical in your life, then you can be sure of one thing: God the Father will take you to His woodshed. My friend, God does not want to be everlastingly taking you to the woodshed. That is why He asks you to come out from among them, to be separate, not to touch the unclean thing. Then God can have an intimate relationship with you as a Father with a son.

CHAPTER 7

THEME: *God's comfort in the heart of Paul*

This is the last chapter in the section on the comfort of God. This is God's comfort in the very heart of Paul, a very personal and a very wonderful chapter.

As a background for this chapter we need to remember that there had been a man in the church in Corinth who had been guilty of gross immorality. He had had an incestuous and adulterous relationship with his own father's wife, his stepmother. The church hadn't dealt with that situation, and Paul had reprimanded them in his first epistle and had said they must deal with it. Now as Paul is writing his second letter to them, they had dealt with this man with the result that he repented and confessed his sin. The church had been accurate in dealing with him. Paul's letter had had the right kind of effect. Titus came to Paul with the report that this man had been weeping over his sin and that he felt utterly unworthy of further recognition by the church. It is to this matter that Paul is referring.

> **Having therefore these promises, dearly beloved, let us cleanse ourselves from all filthiness of the flesh and spirit, perfecting holiness in the fear of God [2 Cor. 7:1].**

What promises is he talking about? He is referring to those at the end of chapter 6. God has said that if we will obey Him, He will be a real Father to us, we will be real sons and daughters to Him, and He can deal with us in that relationship. This does not say that if we don't come out and be separate, we will lose our salvation. It does mean that if we do not lead a clean life, God can't treat us as a Father would want to treat His child. I gave the illustration of the father of the wayward son who said, "I'd like to treat him like my son but I cannot. He is alienated from me and he is in trouble and difficulty. He resents me and I can't be a father to him." He *was* the father of the boy, but he couldn't *act* like a father. God wants to treat us as a Father. A great many of us do not know by *experience* what a wonderful Father we have. We don't give Him a chance to be a real Father to us. What can we do to change that? Paul tells us, "Having therefore these promises, dearly beloved, let us cleanse ourselves." How can we cleanse ourselves? We cannot cleanse our own conscience from the guilt of sin. I am unable to wash out the stain of a guilty conscience, but God has done that through the death of Christ and the shedding of His blood. After we have been cleansed from our sins by the blood of Christ, our hearts still need a daily cleansing from the contamination of each day. When I receive the Word in faith and I act upon that Word, I am cleansed from all the filthiness of the flesh and spirit. This is what the Lord Jesus meant when He said, "Sanctify them through thy truth: thy word is truth" (John 17:17). The best bar of soap in the world is the Word of God. It will really clean us up. The Holy Spirit enables us to deal with the sin in our lives.

Paul says we are to cleanse ourselves from all filthiness of the flesh and of the spirit. All sin is filthiness in the sight of God. Then what is the difference between the sins of the flesh and the sins of the spirit?

The filthiness of the flesh are those sins which we commit in the body. This has to do with unholy lusts, unbridled appetites, drunkenness, gluttony, licentiousness, inordinate affection. These are the sins of the flesh. These are the dirty things. You and I need to be aware of the fact that we are living in a world today that is giving a respectability to the sins of the flesh.

An illustration of this is the attitude of the world toward liquor. Most people today say that alcohol is all right. It is well advertised in the media. The other day I heard an advertisement which said, "The mark of a mature, sensible, and successful man today is one who is able to drink cocktails." What propaganda! What brainwashing of the people! No political dictator has done a more thorough job. The liquor interests do a fantastic amount of brainwashing. But wait a minute! The ad which I was quoting was not for Southern Comfort or Old Crow or some other brand of whiskey. It was an advertisement from an organization which deals with alcoholics. They added, "There are some people who just don't know how to handle their liquor." I'll say there are! There are a whole lot of them—several million of them—and we, the taxpayers, are paying the hospital bills that the liquor interests create. This is an example of the sins of the flesh.

What does the Bible say about this? Listen to Habakkuk 2:15: "Woe unto him that giveth his neighbour drink, that puttest thy bottle to him, and makest him drunken also, that thou mayest look on their nakedness!" God have mercy on you if you serve cocktails in your home and tempt your neighbor to drunkenness. The Word of God rebukes that.

Another illustration of the filthiness of the flesh is the bookstands filled with the vilest pornographic literature that is imaginable which glorifies the human body and sex. In this permissive society God's Word still condemns the sins of the flesh. If you as a Christian are going to indulge in them, my friend, then God cannot act toward you as your Father. Although you may actually be His son, He cannot treat you as a Father would like to treat His son.

Now Paul mentions the filthiness of the spirit. What are some of those sins? Well, how about gossip, my friend? How about vicious slander against some Christian brother? There are a great many people who would never take a gun and pull the trigger to shoot a man down, but they will take the dagger of gossip and put it in his back when he is not listening. Some of the dear saints in the church engage in that kind of practice.

There are the secret sins of the spirit such as vanity and pride. Conceit, haughtiness, unbelief, and covetousness are the dirty sins of the spirit. There are a lot of saints in the church who live by a series of "don'ts"—don't drink, don't smoke, don't play cards. Not one of them would have a cigarette on the end of his tongue, but the words on the end of his tongue burn more deeply than a cigarette could burn. These are some of the sins of the spirit.

Now Paul says that we should "cleanse ourselves from all filthiness of the flesh and spirit, perfecting holiness in the fear of God." The writer to the Hebrews puts it this way: "And make straight paths for your feet, lest that which is lame be turned out of the way; but let it rather be healed. Follow peace with all men, and holiness, without which no man shall see the Lord" (Heb. 12:13–14). Christ is my righteousness. Christ is my holiness. The problem is that my life and His perfection are really far apart. God says we are not to have such a big holiness gap. He wants us to be holy in our lives.

> **Receive us; we have wronged no man, we have corrupted no man, we have defrauded no man [2 Cor. 7:2].**

Paul assures them that he has corrupted no man. He has defrauded no man. He didn't come to them to take up offerings for all sorts of projects. I wish a great many Christians could say the same thing. I feel that sometimes things are not done correctly by the deacon boards in our churches. I think that if a person makes a donation for a specific purpose, it is the duty of the deacon board to make sure the money is used for that specific purpose. They do not have the liberty to say, "Oh, we'll just put this in the general fund," or, "We think it would be more important to use this to retire our debt on a building." Paul could assure them that he had wronged no man, corrupted no man, defrauded no man.

> **I speak not this to condemn you: for I have said before, that ye are in our hearts to die and live with you [2 Cor. 7:3].**

Paul loved these Christians. They were constantly on his heart.

> **Great is my boldness of speech toward you, great is my glorying of you: I am filled with comfort, I am exceeding joyful in all our tribulation [2 Cor. 7:4].**

Now he tells them that he is comforted and is filled with joy. He goes on to give the reason for this.

> **For, when we were come into Macedonia, our flesh had no rest, but we were troubled on every side; without were fightings, within were fears.**

Nevertheless God, that comforteth those that are cast down, comforted us by the coming of Titus;

And not by his coming only, but by the consolation wherewith he was comforted in you, when he told us your earnest desire, your mourning, your fervent mind toward me; so that I rejoiced the more.

For though I made you sorry with a letter, I do not repent, though I did repent: for I perceive that the same epistle hath made you sorry, though it were but for a season.

Now I rejoice, not that ye were made sorry, but that ye sorrowed to repentance: for ye were made sorry after a godly manner, that ye might receive damage by us in nothing [2 Cor. 7:5–9].

Now this is quite lovely, and the background will help us appreciate what he is saying. Remember that in Paul's first epistle to them he wrote a very sharp letter. He called them "babes" and "carnal." He pointed out the gross immorality among them, and he commanded them to deal with it and put it away. And they did deal with it as Paul had instructed them. When Titus arrived in Philippi to join Paul, he brought the news that the church in Corinth had dealt with the situation and that the guilty man had repented of his gross immorality. So Paul wrote in the second chapter of this second epistle that now they should forgive him and comfort him so that he wouldn't be swallowed up in sorrow. He is to be taken back into the fellowship.

After he had left Ephesus, he had gone to Troas, and there he waited, but Titus didn't come. Then he began to rebuke himself. He thought, *Maybe I shouldn't have written such a sharp letter to them after all. Or maybe I should have gone to them directly.* He went on to Philippi, and it was there that Titus met him and brought him word from Corinth.

Someone is going to say to me, "I thought that the Scripture is verbally inspired and that Paul was writing by inspiration of the Holy

Spirit when he wrote to the Corinthians." That is correct. This is the inspired Word of God. I believe that with all my heart. How is it then that Paul was rebuking himself? It was because Paul was human. God had him write like that to let you and me know how human he really was. Also it shows us how tender and sweet and loving he was and that you and I ought to be the same way. What a lesson in this for us! Once Paul had received the news he could write, "I am filled with comfort, I am exceeding joyful in all our tribulation."

It is possible that someone reading this page should sit down and write a letter to an individual whom he hurt years ago. If that someone is you, tell him that you are sorry and want to make things right. Do you know what you would do for him? You would make him exceedingly joyful. We all need to do more of that.

Paul gets very personal when he says, "When we were come into Macedonia, our flesh had no rest, but we were troubled on every side; without were fightings, within were fears." This is so personal I almost feel that we shouldn't read it. But God used a man to comfort Paul: "Nevertheless God, that comforteth those that are cast down, comforted us by the coming of Titus."

You could help some dear saint of God and be a comfort to him. My friend, when was the last time you went to your preacher and put your arm on his shoulder and said, "Brother, I've been praying for you. I see that you are working hard and standing for the things of God, and I just want you to know I am standing with you." He would appreciate that.

Paul continues: "And not by his [Titus'] coming only, but by the consolation wherewith he was comforted in you, when he told us your earnest desire, your mourning, your fervent mind toward me; so that I rejoiced the more." In other words, "You comforted Titus and Titus comforted me."

The other day I was in a church service and a man came to me and said, "My brother who lives back East wrote me. He says that he has been listening by radio to that fellow McGee from California and that, if ever I should meet him, I should tell him that my brother accepted Christ as his Savior." Now I don't know why that man's brother didn't write to me and tell me that, but he didn't. He wrote to his brother and his brother told me. I want to say to you that I was *comforted* by that. It made me know that my radio program is something that I should continue.

The Corinthians had said nice things about Paul. Friend, don't be so hesitant to say something nice about someone else. Really, your tongue won't fall out if you say some nice things.

"For though I made you sorry with a letter, I do not repent, though I did repent: for I perceive that the same epistle hath made you sorry, though it were but for a season. Now I rejoice, not that ye were made sorry, but that ye sorrowed to repentance." You see, repentance and the shedding of tears are not the same. "For ye were made sorry after a *godly* manner, that ye might receive damage by us in nothing."

> **For godly sorrow worketh repentance to salvation not to be repented of: but the sorrow of the world worketh death [2 Cor. 7:10].**

Here we find God's definition of repentance—real repentance. Repentance is a change of mind. As far as I can tell, the only repentance God asks of the lost is in the word *believe.* Believe on the Lord Jesus Christ! What happens when one believes? There is a change of mind. There is a turning from something to Someone. Listen to what Paul wrote to the Thessalonians: ". . . how ye turned to God from idols . . ." (1 Thess. 1:9)—that was a change of mind. How did it come about? They first turned to Christ. When Paul had come to them, he hadn't preached against idolatry, he had preached Christ to them. And they turned to Christ. But they were idolaters. So when they turned to Christ in faith, what else happened? They turned *from* the idols, and that turning from idols was repentance. That is the repentance of the unsaved; it is the repentance to salvation. I don't know if God wants us to emphasize repentance to the unsaved; He does want us to emphasize Christ. When they respond to Christ, there will be a turning from their old unbelief to Christ.

However, God does emphasize repentance for the believer if he is going in the wrong direction, walking in sin. For him there is to be a turning, a repentance. A lot of people simply shed tears, which may not indicate true repentance. That kind of sorrow is the sorrow of the world and works death. True repentance is godly sorrow, which "worketh repentance to salvation not to be repented of"—that is, repentance without regret.

My dad used to tell about a boat on the Mississippi River that had a little bitty boiler and a great big whistle. When it would blow its whistle while going upstream, the boat would start to drift downstream because the boiler was so small it couldn't propel the boat and blow the whistle at the same time. There are a lot of folk who have a great big whistle and a little bitty boiler. They shed a lot of tears and make a big display, but there is no real repentance. They shed tears, but they keep on going in the same direction.

But with these Corinthian believers their repentance was real.

> **For behold this selfsame thing, that ye sorrowed after a godly sort, what carefulness it wrought in you, yea, what clearing of yourselves, yea, what indignation, yea, what fear, yea, what vehement desire, yea, what zeal, yea, what revenge! In all things ye have approved yourselves to be clear in this matter.**
>
> **Wherefore, though I wrote unto you, I did it not for his cause that had done the wrong, nor for his cause that suffered wrong, but that our care for you in the sight of God might appear unto you.**
>
> **Therefore we were comforted in your comfort: yea, and exceedingly the more joyed we for the joy of Titus, because his spirit was refreshed by you all [2 Cor. 7:11–13].**

He commends them for the fact that they really repented.

> **For if I have boasted any thing to him of you, I am not ashamed; but as we spake all things to you in truth, even so our boasting, which I made before Titus, is found a truth.**

And his inward affection is more abundant toward you, whilst he remembereth the obedience of you all, how with fear and trembling ye received him.

I rejoice therefore that I have confidence in you in all things [2 Cor. 7:14–16].

Paul has opened his heart and has shown his inmost feelings. He is full of joy and rejoicing. He has been comforted. This has been God's comfort in the heart of Paul.

CHAPTER 8

THEME: Example of Christian giving

The subject now changes. For the previous seven chapters Paul has talked of the comfort of God. I trust it has brought comfort and strength to you to know that you have a Helper in your Christian life. Our natural reaction is to say, "Paul, go on—tell us more about comfort." However, he changes the subject abruptly. He now talks about the collection for the poor saints of Jerusalem. He brings us back to earth with a thump! The subject changes from Christian *living* to Christian *giving*, which is as vital a part as living.

This section, which includes chapters 8 and 9, divides this way:
1. *Example* of Christian Giving, chapter 8:1–6
2. *Exhortation* to Christian Giving, chapter 8:7–15
3. *Explanation* of Christian Giving, chapters 8:16—9:5
4. *Encouragement* to Christian Giving, chapter 9:6–15

During my twenty-one years as a pastor in downtown Los Angeles I do not think that I preached more than three messages on giving, yet we saw the giving double and triple several times during that period. This confirms my belief that God's people will support a ministry that teaches and preaches the Word of God. I resent the high-pressure promotion and money-raising schemes which are being used in Christian work. I do not think they are scriptural by any means.

These two chapters give us the most extended and complete section on Christian giving that we have in the Scriptures. Actually, all we need to know is here. There are no rules, but there are certain clear-cut principles for giving. That may strike you as being unusual. Someone may say, "I thought we were to give a tithe." No, that is not the rule for today. It might be a principle that you would like to follow, but it is not a rule for anyone today.

The word that is important in this section is the word *grace*. In this chapter the word *grace* occurs seven times, and it occurs three times in chapter 9—ten times in these two chapters. The subject is the grace of giving.

EXAMPLE OF CHRISTIAN GIVING

Moreover, brethren, we do you to wit of the grace of God bestowed on the churches of Macedonia [2 Cor. 8:1].

I want to spend a little time here on that word *grace*. We find it here in the first verse. We find it again in the fourth verse: "Praying us with much entreaty that we would receive the gift, and take upon us the fellowship of the ministering to the saints." The word *gift* in our translation is actually "grace." Another way of translation would be, "Praying us with much entreaty that we would give effect to the grace and fellowship of the service to the saints." The word appears again in the sixth verse: "Insomuch that we desired Titus, that as he had begun, so he would also finish in you the same grace also."

He is calling giving a grace. It is a grace of God. It is a disposition created by the Spirit of God. He is writing to the Corinthians and is telling them that the Macedonians had that kind of grace, and he is hoping that the Corinthians will have that same grace.

The theologian defines grace as the unmerited favor of God. I agree with that, and yet it does not adequately describe this word. It may cause you to miss the rich flavor of it. I studied classical Greek before I studied Koiné, the Greek of the Scriptures, and I found that the Greek word *charis* means an outward grace like beauty or loveliness or charm or kindness or goodwill or gratitude or delight or pleasure. The Greeks had three graces: good, fine, noble. The Greeks were missionary-minded about their culture, and they wanted to impart this to others.

The Holy Spirit chose this word, gave it a new luster and a new glory, and the Christian writers adopted it. Paul uses it again and again. Now notice carefully this definition: The grace of God is the passion of God to share all His goodness with others. Grace means that God wants to bestow upon you good things, goodnesses. He wants to make you fine and noble, and He wants to bring you into the likeness of His Son. This is the grace of which Paul writes in Ephesians: "For by grace are ye saved through faith; and that not of yourselves: it is the gift of God: Not of works, lest any man should boast" (Eph. 2:8–9). We were lost sinners; we had nothing to offer God for our salvation; so He saved us by grace. He had a passion for wanting to save us. He loved us, but He could not arbitrarily forgive us because He is a holy God. He had to provide a way, and that way was that He sent His Son to die for us. We are told that "God so loved the world that he gave his only begotten Son" (see John 3:16). God is in the business of giving, not receiving. We need to make that very clear.

I think sometimes we give the impression that God is poor and that He needs our gifts. He doesn't. God is not poor. He says, "For every beast of the forest is mine, and the cattle upon a thousand hills. I know all the fowls of the mountains: and the wild beasts of the field are mine. If I were hungry, I would not tell thee: for the world is mine, and the fulness thereof" (Ps. 50:10–12). God doesn't get hungry. Even if He did, He would not tell us! God is not in need of anything.

The early church considered giving to be a grace. It was a passion, an overwhelming desire to share the things of God with others.

Paul is writing specifically of a local situation, and we need to recognize that. The Jerusalem church had been the first to give out the gospel—the gospel had begun there. Jesus had told the disciples they should be witnesses unto Him beginning in Jerusalem. The apostles loved Jerusalem, and they locked their arms around their beloved city until persecution drove them from it, scattered them abroad, sent them down the highways into Judea and Samaria and finally to the uttermost parts of the earth. The church in Jerusalem was weakened because of persecution. In fact, there was famine going on, and the church was poverty-stricken.

Now as Paul went about on his third missionary journey, he collected an offering for the church in Jerusalem. That is rather revolutionary. Here the mission churches are sending an offering to help the mother church. Today it is just the opposite. The home church sends out missionaries and supports them out in the foreign field. But in Paul's day the foreign field was supporting the home church.

Paul was not yet able to come to Corinth; so in this letter he sends instructions to them about how to give. Because he intends to come to Corinth, he tells them that he doesn't want any kind of promotion for giving—he doesn't want to be taking up a collection while he is there. He doesn't want to spend time talking about money after he gets there. This collection was to be done beforehand and then, when he arrived, he could spend his time teaching them the Word of God.

What a contrast that is to the usual method today. The usual invitation that I receive is to come over and hold a meeting and while I am there a love offering will be taken for me. If it were done as Paul suggested, a love offering would be taken before an evangelist or a Bible teacher came to speak.

Now I have given to you the color of the local situation and the background of the instructions in this epistle. The *facts* of the local situation have now passed into history, but the *principles* which Paul lays down abide. I believe they are as sharp and fresh today as they were when Paul first gave them.

In the first verse Paul cited the Macedonian believers as examples in Christian giving—this referred to the church at Philippi. In verse 2 he lists their motives and methods of giving.

> **How that in a great trial of affliction the abundance of their joy and their deep poverty abounded unto the riches of their liberality [2 Cor. 8:2].**

Notice that the Macedonians gave out of their "deep poverty." They didn't have riches. They didn't give of their surplus or of their abundance; they gave out of their poverty. I'm afraid we don't know much about that kind of giving today.

> **For to their power, I bear record, yea, and beyond their power they were willing of themselves;**
>
> **Praying us with much entreaty that we would receive the gift, and take upon us the fellowship of the ministering to the saints [2 Cor. 8:3–4].**

It would be more accurate to translate this: "Praying us with much entreaty that we would receive the grace"—that gift they had taken up was a grace, and it was fellowship, which means it was a sharing of the things of Christ.

You and I cannot realize the love that they had one for another. We talk about social action in the church today; I must confess that we have almost lost sight of it in our fundamental churches. It is a wonderful thing to give to the missions, but must we neglect folk in our own congregations who are in need? Many of them don't even want their needs to be known in the local congregation because they know it would become a subject of gossip in the church. They don't want to accept help because they feel it would be more or less a disgrace. I've discovered this in my own ministry. Sometimes I could not reveal the name of the person in need to a committee or a group that wanted to know to whom the help was going, because the committee would not keep it in confidence, and by the time it got to their wives, it would be throughout the church. We have lost today this wonderful grace of giving.

Now notice what the believers in Macedonia had done—this is unusual.

And this they did, not as we hoped, but first gave their own selves to the Lord, and unto us by the will of God [2 Cor. 8:5].

Paul says this was not something that he had expected. First of all, they had given themselves to the Lord. That is basic. Secondly, they had given themselves, apparently to some local work of Christ and they were sold out to it. They gave themselves to Paul by the will of God, which means they helped him to get out the gospel. You see, they were sold out to God.

Back in Paul's first letter to the Corinthians he wrote about the Resurrection and heaven (see ch. 15), and they were about to say, "Brother Paul, tell us more about heaven." Then Paul shook them right down to their shoestrings by saying, "Now concerning the collection for the saints, as I have given order to the churches of Galatia, even so do ye" (1 Cor. 16:1). He wanted to talk to them about something very practical. And he tells them here in his second letter that they are not to give grudgingly. The Macedonian believers gave out of "the abundance of their joy and their deep poverty." What a picture! God loves a cheerful giver, and we see it in shoeleather here—it was a fellowship. They shared what they had.

They owed the home church in Jerusalem for all their spiritual blessings. They had received the gospel from them. Now they were returning material gifts to the home church which was in such a sad situation. Paul writes in Galatians 6:6: "Let him that is taught in the word communicate unto him that teacheth in all good things." That literally means, "Pay the preacher." It means, my friend, that you ought to support the work from which you derive a spiritual blessing.

A man, living out of fellowship with the Lord, heard our radio messages and the Word of God brought him back to the Lord. We have a building which belongs to "Thru the Bible" because he gave that building to us. He gave it hilariously. He gave it joyously. That is the way it should be given. It should be out of the abundance of joy. We are never to give reluctantly or because we think we ought to give. We should have a passion to give so that the Word of God can reach others.

You remember that the Lord Jesus stood aside and watched the people give in the temple—I think He still does that. The rich came in and gave large gifts, but the poor little widow came and put in her two mites. The Lord said she had cast in more than they all (see Mark 12:41–44). She gave of her poverty and she gave all that she had. If you measured the value of those little coppers against the riches of that temple, they didn't amount to anything. But the Lord Jesus gives God's evaluation: "And he said, Of a truth I say unto you, that this poor widow hath cast in more than they all: For all these have of their abundance cast in unto the offerings of God: but she of her penury hath cast in all the living that she had" (Luke 21:3–4).

It has been said, "When it comes to giving, some people stop at nothing." That is where a great many folk stop.

The story is told of a Scottish church that was attempting to raise money for a new building. One member of the church was a rich Scot who was known to be worth fifty thousand pounds. He was a typical Scot and was pretty stingy, like most of us are. A deacon came to see him and asked, "Brother, how much are you going to give for the new church?" The Scot replied, "Oh, I guess I'll be able to put in the widow's mite." The deacon called out in the next meeting, "Brethren, we have all the money we need. This brother is going to give fifty thousand pounds." The man was amazed. "I didn't say I would give fifty thousand pounds; I said I would give the widow's mite." The deacon replied, "Well, she gave her all, and I thought that is what you meant to give!" It is interesting that God notes what you give but also what you keep for yourself.

In another church they were taking up an offering for a building program. The man calling on one of the members said to him, "How much are you going to give, brother?" "Well," he said, "I guess I could give ten dollars and not feel it." The man replied, "Then why don't you make it twenty dollars and *feel* it?" You see, the blessing only comes when you feel it, my friend. This is the meaning of "It is more blessed to give than to receive."

The Macedonian believers gave themselves to God. And, my friend, if God doesn't have you, He doesn't want anything from you. If God doesn't have the hand, He doesn't want the gift that is in the hand.

Insomuch that we desired Titus, that as he had begun, so he would also finish in you the same grace also [2 Cor. 8:6].

Paul says that the grace which motivated the Macedonians should be the same grace that would motivate the Corinthians. The real test of any person lies in what he gives. Someone has said there are three books that are essential for a worship service: the first book is the Bible, the second is the hymn book, and the third is the pocketbook. Giving is a part of our worship to God. If we do not have the grace of giving, we should pray to God and ask Him to give us a generous, sharing spirit.

EXHORTATION TO CHRISTIAN GIVING

Therefore, as ye abound in every thing, in faith, and utterance, and knowledge, and in all diligence, and in your love to us, see that ye abound in this grace also [2 Cor. 8:7].

Paul is commending them. They abound in faith; they were able to witness; they had knowledge and diligence; and they had love for Paul and for the other apostles. Now he asks them to abound in this grace also. What does he refer to? He means the grace of giving.

I speak not by commandment, but by occasion of the forwardness of others, and to prove the sincerity of your love [2 Cor. 8:8].

Paul is saying here that giving today is not by law, by rote, or by ritual. I know that there are good Bible expositors who say we are to give the tithe. Obviously, the tithe was basic back in the Old Testament. However, if you examine it very carefully, you will find that the people gave three tithes. One was actually for the support of the government, which would be what we call taxes today. So the "tithe" is not the basis on which Christians are to give. Paul says, "I speak not by commandment." He is not asking the Corinthians to give because it is a commandment.

Paul gives two reasons by which he is asking them to give. The first is "by occasion of the forwardness of others"—which would be the example which the Macedonians had given. The second reason is to "prove the sincerity of your love." It is still true today that the pocketbook is really the test of a man's love. It is the most sensitive area of a Christian.

For ye know the grace of our Lord Jesus Christ, that, though he was rich, yet for your sakes he became poor, that ye through his poverty might be rich [2 Cor. 8:9].

If you are looking for a standard for giving, here it is: the Lord Jesus Christ Himself. He was rich but He became poor. He came down here and took a place of poverty. Imagine leaving heaven and coming down to this earth to be born in Bethlehem, to live in Nazareth, to die on a cross outside the walls of Jerusalem, and to be put into the darkness of a tomb! He was rich but He became poor for you and me.

> **And herein I give my advice: for this is expedient for you, who have begun before, not only to do, but also to be forward a year ago [2 Cor. 8:10].**

This indicates that the Corinthians had made a pledge or a promise and had begun to give for this collection a year earlier. This raises the issue of making a pledge to give a certain amount of money. Some people say they don't think a Christian should make a pledge. I think we need to recognize that we sign pledges for everything else, and I think that people ought to be willing to make a pledge to God's work. We promise to pay our rent; we sign notes when we buy an automobile or a refrigerator. I say that we can sign on the dotted line for God's work, too.

> **Now therefore perform the doing of it; that as there was a readiness to will, so there may be a performance also out of that which ye have [2 Cor. 8:11].**

Paul is saying they should carry through with their pledge. They should put their money where their mouth is. However, remember that this is not a commandment. We are not commanded to make a pledge. However, this verse does tell us that if we do make a pledge, then we are to carry it through and perform it.

> **For if there be first a willing mind, it is accepted according to that a man hath, and not according to that he hath not [2 Cor. 8:12].**

Here is something very important to note. Each should give according to "that a man hath," and he is to do it with a willing mind. No one is to give according to what he does not have.

In the section on 1 Corinthians, I gave an illustration which I will repeat because it is a very fine example of this principle.

When I was pastoring a church in Texas, one of my officers owned several Coca-Cola plants, and one of them was in our town. He was a man of means, and he owned a ranch where we used to go out to hunt and fish. Often he would ask me why I didn't preach on tithing. One day I said, "Why should I preach on tithing?" He said, "Because it is the Bible way of giving." I agreed, "Yes, it was the Old Testament way of giving, but under grace I don't believe tithing is the way it should be done." So he asked me, "How do you think it ought to be done?" I took him to this verse: "As God has prospered him." Now this was during the Depression. If you are as old as I am, you will remember that the Depression in the 1930s was a very serious time. So I said to him, "For some strange reason, Coca-Cola is selling, and you are doing very well. However, there are some members in our church who couldn't give a tithe right now. I don't believe God is asking them to give a tenth. There are a few people who are doing well, and they are to give as they have been prospered—and they are not to stop with a tenth. Probably they ought to give a half." Do you know that this man never again suggested that I preach on tithing! The reason was that he found out that a man is to give according to what he hath, not according to what he hath not.

The tithes were a basic measurement in the Old Testament, and I cannot believe that any Christian today who has a good income should give less than one tenth. In this time of great abundance Christians should be giving more than a tenth.

For I mean not that other men be eased, and ye burdened [2 Cor. 8:13].

Paul is saying that a burden should not be placed on anyone.

But by an equality, that now at this time your abundance may be a supply for their want, that their abundance also may be a supply for your want: that there may be equality [2 Cor. 8:14].

Perhaps you have been blessed with a good automobile, a lovely home, nice furniture, and all the appliances that are considered necessary in our contemporary culture. May I say to you that God expects you to share in the Lord's work. You may be like my rancher friend who would like to settle for the tithe. He wanted me to preach on the tithe so he would feel comfortable in his giving. After I had talked with him, I don't think he ever felt comfortable about his tithe-giving. Those who are able to give should give, and we should not burden those who are unable to give.

As it is written, He that had gathered much had nothing over; and he that had gathered little had no lack [2 Cor. 8:15].

Paul gives the example of the gathering of the manna in the wilderness. Each was to gather enough for one day. Some man might go out with several baskets and say, "Let's just fill them up. I'll gather bushel baskets of manna while I can." He would go out and greedily gather up much more than he needed. What would happen? After he had eaten what he needed for that day, he would find that all the rest had spoiled by the next morning. It was God's plan that each one should have just enough and no more.

We will learn in chapter 9, verse 6, that ". . . He which soweth sparingly shall reap also sparingly; and he which soweth bountifully shall reap also bountifully." I think that God will begin to deal with you as you have been dealing with Him. I think that God keeps books. He does not put us under law because He wants our giving to be a grace, a passion, a desire to share. It should be a joyful experience. You ought to be able to say to other folk, "You ought to listen to Dr. McGee. He's talking about the most wonderful privilege in the world.

He is telling us how we can be happy by giving." That may sound crazy to you, but that is exactly what Paul is saying here.

EXPLANATION OF CHRISTIAN GIVING

But thanks be to God, which put the same earnest care into the heart of Titus for you [2 Cor. 8:16].

"Thanks" is the same Greek word *charis*, which has been translated "grace." Although "thanks" is a good translation, it would be equally correct to translate it "grace be to God."

Paul is saying that he sent Titus to get their offering, but it was already a grace in his heart. Titus wanted as much as Paul did to take up an offering for the poor saints in Jerusalem.

For indeed he accepted the exhortation; but being more forward, of his own accord he went unto you.

And we have sent with him the brother, whose praise is in the gospel throughout all the churches;

And not that only, but who was also chosen of the churches to travel with us with this grace, which is administered by us to the glory of the same Lord, and declaration of your ready mind [2 Cor. 8:17–19].

You see, Titus and his companion had this grace in their hearts. The giving was to be for the glory of God. Whatever we give, my friend, should be for the glory of God.

Avoiding this, that no man should blame us in this abundance which is administered by us [2 Cor. 8:20].

Paul is saying, "We are going to be honest in the use of the money we collect from you and in the way we handle it."

Providing for honest things, not only in the sight of the Lord, but also in the sight of men [2 Cor. 8:21].

This is one of the more sensitive areas in the Lord's work. Many Christian organizations and churches major in heavy promotion to encourage giving to a certain work. No effort—or at best, *little* effort—is made to tell how the money is used. There should be the presentation of tangible evidence that the money is used to give out the Word of God and that there are results that can be documented—not just isolated cases. There should be confidence in the organization to which we give, that it is honest and is operated on the highest level of integrity. We should not support an organization about which we have doubts. We must remember that this is a big, bad world and that there are religious racketeers in it. We need to beware.

Even Paul, this great apostle, says, "Providing for honest things, not only in the sight of the Lord, but also in the sight of men." It should be obvious that the money is being used for the purpose for which it is given.

And we have sent with them our brother, whom we have oftentimes proved diligent in many things, but now much more diligent, upon the great confidence which I have in you.

Whether any do inquire of Titus, he is my partner and fellow-helper concerning you: or our brethren be inquired of, they are the messengers of the churches, and the glory of Christ [2 Cor. 8:22–23].

They can trust Titus. He will make a good report. They can trust Paul who will also report to them. The money will be not be delivered by just one person.

Wherefore shew ye to them, and before the churches, the proof of your love, and of our boasting on your behalf [2 Cor. 8:24].

Paul is asking for proof of their love. You see, friend, if you really mean business, there will be more than verbiage. Giving will be a tangible expression of your love.

I'm afraid there are a great many Christians who are like the young fellow who wrote to his girl: "I would cross the widest ocean for you. I'd swim the deepest river for you. I would scale the highest mountain for you. I'd crawl across the burning sands of the desert for you." Then he concluded with a P.S.: "If it doesn't rain Wednesday night, I'll be over to see you." A great many of us like to talk about how we love Jesus, but we are not willing to sacrifice much for Him.

Paul is urging the Corinthians to show the *proof* of their love.

CHAPTER 9

THEME: Collection for the poor saints at Jerusalem

This chapter continues directly with the same subject which we had in chapter 8. There it was the *grace* of giving; now we have before us what Christian giving *is*.

EXPLANATION OF CHRISTIAN GIVING
(Continued)

For as touching the ministering to the saints, it is superfluous for me to write to you:

For I know the forwardness of your mind, for which I boast of you to them of Macedonia, that Achaia was ready a year ago; and your zeal hath provoked very many.

Yet have I sent the brethren, lest our boasting of you should be in vain in this behalf; that, as I said, ye may be ready:

Lest haply if they of Macedonia come with me, and find you unprepared, we (that we say not, ye) should be ashamed in this same confident boasting [2 Cor. 9:1–4].

Paul says that he would be very embarrassed if he came over there, having boasted of them to other folk, and then found out they hadn't given anything. Liberal giving is a real test of any church. I go to some churches that have real spiritual vigor; they are great churches, and I have found out that they are generous in their giving. I have also been to some churches that are really dead spiritually. And I have discovered that they don't give much either. They are dead in their giving, too. The size of the offering is a pretty good barometer.

Now you see that these Corinthian Christians had made a pledge that they would give something toward the relief of believers in Jerusalem. May I say here that any pledge that a Christian makes is between that person and the Lord. It is a pledge to the Lord that you will do something or that you will give something.

I know a wealthy man who was asked, "How in the world did you become so rich when you give so much away?" "Well," he answered, "The Lord shovels it in and I shovel it out, and God has the bigger shovel." My friend, we can never outgive God.

> **Therefore I thought it necessary to exhort the brethren, that they would go before unto you, and make up beforehand your bounty, whereof ye had notice before, that the same might be ready, as a matter of bounty, and not as of covetousness [2 Cor. 9:5].**

You will notice that the gift is called a bounty. That indicates that it would be a generous gift, which is the evidence of the grace of God working in the heart.

ENCOURAGEMENT TO CHRISTIAN GIVING

> **But this I say, He which soweth sparingly shall reap also sparingly; and he which soweth bountifully shall reap also bountifully [2 Cor. 9:6].**

When Paul was talking to the Ephesian elders, he reminded them of this same thing. "I have shewed you all things, how that so labouring ye ought to support the weak, and to remember the words of the Lord Jesus, how he said, It is more blessed to give than to receive" (Acts 20:35). Apparently, "it is more blessed to give than to receive" was an expression which the Lord Jesus used constantly. I know that this has become a very trite bromide today. It is quoted a great deal and practiced very little.

The word *blessed* actually means "happy." It will make you happier to give than to receive. How does it affect you when you give?

Here is an acid test for you and for me today. Do we sow sparingly? Do we give in that way? Suppose a farmer would sow a bushel of grain on a particular plot of ground and reap an abundant harvest. Suppose he would say the next year, "There is no use wasting a bushel of grain on this ground this year; I will save *half* a bushel for myself and sow only half a bushel." Any farmer knows that he would get a very small yield. The principle is that whoever sows sparingly will reap sparingly, and he who sows bountifully will reap bountifully.

When I was speaking at Siloam Springs, Arkansas, some folk came from Oklahoma City. The lady is about my age and she was raised in a little place called Tishomingo, Oklahoma. My father was killed in a cotton gin there and is buried there. In that day it was the custom when there was a death in a family for the neighbors and friends to send food to the bereaved family. I shall never forget the wonderful food that was sent to us at that time. This lady told me that she could recall as a girl that her mother cooked up a great deal of food and sent it over to our house. She said, "I never knew that years later I would be listening to you. We gave you physical food, and now you supply spiritual food for us." They didn't sow sparingly, and I hope they are reaping abundantly. I believe this is a true principle in every area of life. One of the reasons some of us are so poor today is that we are so tight-fisted when we are dealing with the Lord.

Every man according as he purposeth in his heart, so let him give; not grudgingly, or of necessity: for God loveth a cheerful giver [2 Cor. 9:7].

What you feel right down in your heart you *ought* to give, *that* is what you should give. But here is the test: "not grudgingly." God does not want any grudging giving. What does that mean? God does not want one penny from you if you would rather keep it for yourself.

Perhaps you say, "Well, I am an officer in the church and it is my responsibility to give." Or, "I am a member of that church and I feel responsible." It is true that the church may say that to you. As a pastor, I've told people, "This is your church and you ought to support it." But *God* does not say that. He says that if you are going to give grudgingly, He doesn't want it. Not only does God not want it, but I believe that God doesn't use it either.

Not only does it say God does not want you to give if you give grudgingly, neither does He want you to give "of necessity." He doesn't want you to give at all unless you are giving willingly and gladly.

Some folk say, "Well, I had better give because everybody else is giving, and it would look bad if I didn't give something." That is giving of necessity. God does not want that kind of giving.

"God loveth a cheerful giver." That should be the happiest part of the service. I have been in many churches where they take up an offering and then the congregation stands and sings, "Praise God from whom all blessings flow." I think that is wonderful. The only thing that would be better would be if they would sing it first. This would put them in the attitude of giving and of giving joyfully. Also they would be able to reach for their wallets as they stood up! God loves a cheerful giver. If you can't give cheerfully, God doesn't want you to give.

> **And God is able to make all grace abound toward you; that ye, always having all sufficiency in all things, may abound to every good work [2 Cor. 9:8].**

I have never known anyone who has gone broke giving to the Lord's work. There may be some who have, but I have never met them in my ministry. In believe that God will bless you. I don't think the blessings He gives to you will always be material blessings. A great many folk think they can hold God to a promise of material blessings. I don't think you can. He does promise to bless us with all spiritual blessings.

> **(As it is written, He hath dispersed abroad; he hath given to the poor: his righteousness remaineth for ever.**
>
> **Now he that ministereth seed to the sower both minister bread for your food, and multiply your seed sown, and increase the fruits of your righteousness;) [2 Cor. 9:9–10].**

This is a quotation from Psalm 112. It calls the man blessed who fears the Lord and who gives to the poor. We are to share with those who do not have as much. I believe that in the church we ought to take care of our own. There are so many opportunities to share with folk. Many Christians have the *gift* of hospitality—and that is a gift. They have a way of opening their homes and making people feel at home. Often they take folk to church first so they hear the gospel and then have them in their home for dinner afterward. That is a marvelous way of witnessing. It is a way to reach the lonely and those who lack fellowship.

Paul gives the illustration of the farmer who doesn't mind going out to scatter bushel after bushel of seed, because he believes that he will get an abundant harvest. It is God who multiplies the seed of the farmer. It is God who will multiply everything that you do for Him. So don't be afraid to give to the Lord's work.

I had an experience once when I had to encourage a young man *not* to give. He had been recently saved, and he was actually giving so much that he was not keeping enough for his own family. The Bible says that we are worse than the heathen if we do not take care of our own family (see 1 Tim. 5:8). I pointed this out to him and told him that he also needed to care for the necessities of his family, and after that he should give generously to the Lord. God does not want us to be extremists even in this matter of giving. We need to be balanced. We need good, sound, common sense and good, consecrated judgment.

> **Being enriched in every thing to all bountifulness, which causeth through us thanksgiving to God.**
>
> **For the administration of this service not only supplieth the want of the saints, but is abundant also by many thanksgivings unto God [2 Cor. 9:11–12].**

You see, when you give, it will cause people to thank God for you. It is God who will get the praise and the glory.

> **Whiles by the experiment of this ministration they glorify God for your professed subjection unto the gospel of**

Christ, and for your liberal distribution unto them, and unto all men [2 Cor. 9:13].

While I was visiting the mission field in Venezuela a certain missionary there told me about a family that I knew back in Los Angeles. The missionary said, "How generous they have been to me! I thank God for them." That is the way Paul said it would be. Missionaries in Venezuela were thanking God for a family in Los Angeles. Is anyone anywhere thanking God for your generosity?

And by their prayer for you, which long after you for the exceeding grace of God in you [2 Cor. 9:14].

Giving is a grace. We are not commanded to give a tithe. It is not to be something done under law. It is a grace. God asks us to give as a grace according to our circumstances. Some Christians should be giving much more than a tithe. Other Christians are not able to give at all. We are to give as we "are able." Now Paul caps the whole subject of giving by saying:

Thanks be unto God for his unspeakable gift [2 Cor. 9:15].

Regardless of how much you are giving, you cannot give like God gives. He has given an unspeakable gift. No man can approach the gift that God gave in giving His own Son to die. Think of this for a moment. We are back to what was said in chapter 8, verse 9. Though He was rich, He left heaven, left all the glory, came down as a missionary to this world. He came not only to live but to give His life in death for you. He came to be brutally killed in order that you and I might have eternal life. He made His soul a sacrifice for sin for you and for me.

We are told in Hebrews that He did this "for the joy that was set before him" (Heb. 12:2). Oh, my friend, He is the wonderful, glorious Savior! Don't ever bring Him down to a low level. He is the Bright and Morning Star. He is the Son of God who has redeemed us. He is the unspeakable gift to you and me. That is the very apex of giving. No one can go beyond that kind of giving.

CHAPTER 10

THEME: Authentication of Paul's apostleship

Now we come to the last great division of this epistle, which is the calling of the apostle Paul. The first division I have called Christian *living*, the second one I called Christian *giving*, and this one I call Christian *guarding*. It was a radical change when we saw Paul begin to write about Christian giving. Now we come to an altogether new section, and it marks such a radical change in tone and style that many critics have supposed that this is the beginning of a third epistle. Candidly, I cannot accept that theory. The change in tone can be explained easily on another basis.

As we have seen, the church in Corinth was a divided church. Paul said when he first wrote to them, "For it hath been declared unto me of you, my brethren, by them which are of the house of Chloe, that there are contentions among you" (1 Cor. 1:11). The majority of the church respected the authority of Paul. There was a minority who opposed Paul and rejected his authority. It would seem that in the first nine chapters he is addressing the majority. In chapters 10, 11, and 12 he is addressing the minority. It is like changing from daylight to darkness.

In this section we will find the apostle opening his great heart of love—his heart as a missionary and as a human being. We will meet him as we have never met him before because in this section he actually defends his apostleship.

> **Now I Paul myself beseech you by the meekness and gentleness of Christ, who in presence am base among you, but being absent am bold toward you [2 Cor. 10:1].**

You remember that Paul had written a strong letter of correction. The minority criticized him severely, and they were saying, "Paul writes big, but when he is among us he is nobody."

Paul beseeches them by "the meekness and gentleness of Christ."

Paul came to Corinth as a tentmaker. He wasn't chargeable to anyone, and he didn't want to be. He would work in the marketplace all day. He would perspire and his hands would get dirty. He was working there, and he was talking to the multitude as they passed by. Now the Corinthians would say of him, "He's not an apostle. Look at him. He's a tentmaker. He is just an ordinary man." Well, friend, he was an ordinary man, but he happened also to be an apostle. Paul looked just like anyone else. In fact, some people would have looked down on him because he labored with his hands. So when he says, "I Paul myself beseech you by the meekness and gentleness of Christ," he is saying that he is like the Lord when He was here on earth. He says, "Who in presence am base among you." He was not something special to see. He wasn't a somebody. He was just an ordinary fellow making tents. So the Corinthians would be apt to say, "When he is among us, he is base. But when he writes to us, he is bold and writes with authority. Who does he think he is?"

Paul writes in the meekness and the gentleness of Christ. Our Lord didn't lift up His voice to defend Himself. Our Lord was not striking in personal appearance, and He did not look as different as the artists would have us believe. He didn't walk around with a halo around His head. He was meek and lowly, and that is to be the badge of His followers. That is the fraternity pin of believers.

So Paul writes to them and says, "Don't let looks fool you." Paul had the authority of an apostle. Paul had a divine mission. He spoke with authority. He was conscious of supernatural power, and he exercised supernatural power. Paul urges them not to force him to exercise his authority. He would like to come again in meekness and gentleness. He urges them not to think of him simply in the flesh.

I don't think a minister of the gospel today needs to wear a robe or needs to button his collar in the back to prove he is a minister of the Lord Jesus Christ. I believe he can prove it by his life and in the fact that he preaches the Word of God. We still find the same tendency among some people as was present in Corinth. They want to degrade the man who teaches the Word of God. The Devil is very clever in this matter. Right now the Devil does not seem to be attacking the Word of

God. There is a real interest in the Word of God among multitudes of people. So what does the Devil do? He attacks the reputation of the man of God who is preaching the Word of God. This is the way he gets in. He tries to discredit the man. That is exactly what happened to Paul.

I know of a church where the pastor taught the Word of God. There were some members there who didn't like him at all, and when he left the church they attempted to crucify the man. Yet they would tell you they believed the Word of God, and they all carried big Bibles under their arms. They don't really believe the Word of God—in fact, they don't even know what is in it. If a pastor preaches the Word of God and does not cater to such a group, believe me, he is in trouble. That is the Devil's method.

> **But I beseech you, that I may not be bold when I am present with that confidence, wherewith I think to be bold against some, which think of us as if we walked according to the flesh [2 Cor. 10:2].**

Paul is saying to them that they should not think of him as walking according to the flesh because he made tents and his hands got dirty and he was sweaty as he worked. This is the way they had evaluated him.

> **For though we walk in the flesh, we do not war after the flesh [2 Cor. 10:3].**

The Greek word for flesh is *sarx*, and it can be used in three different ways. It can speak of the body, the physical body that we have, the meat that is on the bones. It can speak of weakness, meaning that which is psychological. It can also mean that corrupt nature which you and I have, that fallen nature. That is the spiritual meaning. So this word can be used in a physical sense, in a psychological sense, and in a spiritual sense.

Paul uses the word *flesh* in all three senses but more frequently in the sense of the old Adamic, fallen nature. "For I know that in me (that is, in my flesh,) dwelleth no good thing . . ." (Rom. 7:18). He is referring to the corrupt nature—he is using *flesh* in the spiritual sense.

When he says, "For though we walk in the flesh, we do not war after the flesh," he is using *flesh* in the psychological sense. Paul says that he walked in the flesh—weakness. I do not think that Paul came to Corinth in the energy of the flesh. The warfare was spiritual warfare. In his letter to the Ephesians he wrote, "For we wrestle not against flesh and blood, but against principalities, against powers, against the rulers of the darkness of this world, against spiritual wickedness in high places" (Eph. 6:12).

Paul did not come as an ordinary man who was dependent upon the principles of the natural. Paul didn't come to Corinth to put on a Madison Avenue campaign. He didn't use the methods of advertising and organization in human effort and energy. This does not mean that there is no time for us to use these. I am just saying that Paul didn't use them. He was not one of the "personality boys" who uses cleverness with many quotations and clichés and who soars to heights of beautiful language. He didn't come on an anti-Nero or an anti-Caesar campaign. He didn't come to Corinth to clean up the city. He didn't come at the invitation of the Christians to put on a campaign.

Paul had written in 1 Corinthians 2:2, "For I determined not to know any thing among you, save Jesus Christ, and him crucified." Paul had a grand perspective of an entire battlefield. There was a heaven to gain, and there was a hell to shun. He was in a warfare that was spiritual and that required spiritual weapons.

(For the weapons of our warfare are not carnal, but mighty through God to the pulling down of strong holds;) [2 Cor. 10:4].

This is a parenthesis, and in this verse Paul does not even list the weapons. Spiritual warfare means that we have a spiritual enemy, and a spiritual enemy requires spiritual weapons. We are told that we have some weapons and they are mighty. They are effective. Are you able to identify those spiritual weapons which we need today?

Our first weapon is the *Word of God*. We need to have confidence in the Word of God. It is the sword of the Spirit. Paul could come to Corinth, that citadel of philosophy and religion, with the weapon of the Word of God. That is exactly the weapon that he used. Paul writes in Ephesians, "And take the helmet of salvation, and the sword of the Spirit, which is the word of God" (Eph. 6:17). Paul drew his trusty sword, and he depended upon the naked blade of it. He wrote, "For I am not ashamed of the gospel of Christ: for it is the power of God unto salvation to every one that believeth; to the Jew first, and also to the Greek" (Rom. 1:16).

We, too, need to have confidence in the Word of God. We need to have a firm confidence in the verbal inspiration of the Scriptures. This must be more than just a creed. I listened to a preacher who said he believed in the verbal inspiration of the Bible. He quoted poetry and some cute clichés and some pert epigrams. He had every form of philosophical argument but no exposition of the Word of God. May I say to you, *that* is not confidence in the Word of God, nor is it using the Word as a weapon.

I am conservative in my theology. I believe in the inspiration of the Word of God, which includes the Book of Genesis and especially the account of creation. I believe in hell. In fact, I believe the Bible from the beginning to the end. It is the sword of the Spirit, my friend. It is one of our weapons.

The second weapon is the presence of the *Holy Spirit*. Paul recognized his own human weakness. He knew that he was sealed by the Holy Spirit and empowered by the Holy Spirit.

Another weapon of our warfare is *prayer*. Now it is true that there is very little about prayer in either of the Corinthian epistles. However, Paul certainly believed in prayer. In the Book of Ephesians he lists this as one of the offensive weapons. ". . . and the sword of the Spirit, which is the word of God: Praying always with all prayer and supplication in the Spirit, and watching thereunto with all perseverance and supplication for all saints" (Eph. 6:17–18).

Casting down imaginations, and every high thing that exalteth itself against the knowledge of God, and bring-

ing into captivity every thought to the obedience of Christ [2 Cor. 10:5].

In this spiritual battle the warriors are successful. When I say this, I do not mean they are victorious. God gets the victory. When we are successful, the glory all goes to Him. "Now thanks be unto God, which always causeth us to triumph"—how? "in Christ, and maketh manifest the savour of his knowledge by us in every place" (2 Cor. 2:14). We won't win everyone to Christ, but we can get the Word of God out. Thank God for the open door of witnessing in our day. We are not victorious, but we sure can be successful.

And having in a readiness to revenge all disobedience, when your obedience is fulfilled.

Do ye look on things after the outward appearance? If any man trust to himself that he is Christ's, let him of himself think this again, that, as he is Christ's, even so are we Christ's [2 Cor. 10:6–7].

Speaking to the opposition, Paul says, "We belong to Christ as much as anyone."

For though I should boast somewhat more of our authority, which the Lord hath given us for edification, and not for your destruction, I should not be ashamed [2 Cor. 10:8].

Paul has the authority of an apostle. It is not to destroy them, but for their edification—that is, to build them up in the faith.

That I may not seem as if I would terrify you by letters.

For his letters, say they, are weighty and powerful; but his bodily presence is weak, and his speech contemptible [2 Cor. 10:9–10].

Paul does not want his letters to be bold and terrifying and then he himself to be weak among them. I believe this indicates to us that Paul was not what one would call an attractive man. When people heard Paul, it was obvious to them that he was not preaching to them under his own physical strength or by his eloquence or by his personal magnetism. I think he must have been a weak-looking vessel. Perhaps, as with Samson in the time of the judges, it was obvious that his strength was not within himself but came from the Spirit of God.

Let such an one think this, that, such as we are in word by letters when we are absent, such will we be also in deed when we are present.

For we dare not make ourselves of the number, or compare ourselves with some that commend themselves: but they measuring themselves by themselves, and comparing themselves among themselves, are not wise [2 Cor. 10:11–12].

Paul is injecting a little note of humor. A great many folk compare themselves among themselves, which is the reason that many people in our churches think they have arrived. They feel they are really fine, outstanding, spiritual Christians because they compare themselves with other Christians in their group. That is not the yardstick we are to use, my friend. This is one of the tragedies of the hour. A person can be in a cold church and grow cold himself and yet not be conscious of it because he compares himself with the cold Christians around him. We all need to be around other Christians who challenge us. There are too many Christians who are in some little clique or group or church, and they feel smug and satisfied because they are all in the same boat.

But we will not boast of things without our measure, but according to the measures of the rule which God hath distributed to us, a measure to reach even unto you [2 Cor. 10:13].

The complaint of the Corinthian believers was that Paul would not come to see them. They said he would spend time with others but would not come to Corinth to see them.

How many Christians criticize their pastor because he doesn't spend time visiting with them! They want more and more of his time. My friend, when a pastor spends his time petting and pampering people, he is wasting the Lord's time. He needs to spend his time with those who are desperately in need of help. He also needs to spend time in the Word of God.

> **For we stretch not ourselves beyond our measure, as though we reached not unto you: for we are come as far as to you also in preaching the gospel of Christ:**
>
> **Not boasting of things without our measure, that is, of other men's labours; but having hope, when your faith is increased, that we shall be enlarged by you according to our rule abundantly.**
>
> **To preach the gospel in the regions beyond you, and not to boast in another man's line of things made ready to our hand [2 Cor. 10:14–16].**

Paul tells them they must remember that he came to them first. He was the first one to bring the gospel to them, and he had traveled a long way from home to do that. He tells them that his method is not to come and be a pastor of a church. He had been called to be a missionary. After he would begin a work, he would travel on. He was always moving out to the frontier. He never built on another man's foundation.

> **But he that glorieth, let him glory in the Lord.**
>
> **For not he that commendeth himself is approved, but whom the Lord commendeth [2 Cor. 10:17–18].**

We stand before the Lord for His commending. This is actually a word of warning to us. Don't criticize someone before you find out what his calling from the Lord is. One man may be gifted in personal visitation; another man may be gifted in the pulpit. If you have a man who is gifted in the pulpit, don't criticize him, but give him the necessary time to prepare his messages. If he is doing that, then he cannot be spending his time running around to visit you. Another man may not be a brilliant preacher but may be an excellent organizer. Then that is his gift. Find out what the person's gift is and help that person to exercise his gift. Don't sit in judgment on him if he is not doing everything you think he should do.

Paul is telling the Corinthian believers that he is doing what God had called him to do. He was called to be a missionary, and that is what he is doing.

CHAPTER 11

THEME: Vindication of Paul's apostleship

Paul writes very intimately and very personally in this chapter. Paul reminds these folk that they are joined to the living Christ, and he expresses his deep concern for them. I can certainly say that the message of this epistle has been beneficial to me. I have spent a great deal of time studying it, and I have found it has had a real message to my own heart.

This final section of the Epistle to the Corinthians concerns the calling of the apostle Paul. In chapter 10 we found the authentication of Paul's apostleship. Now we come to a very personal section which is the vindication of Paul's apostleship.

> **Would to God ye could bear with me a little in my folly: and indeed bear with me.**
>
> **For I am jealous over you with godly jealousy: for I have espoused you to one husband, that I may present you as a chaste virgin to Christ [2 Cor. 11:1–2].**

Paul came to Corinth. He preached the gospel. A church came into existence because Paul had espoused these people, these believers, to Christ.

> **But I fear, lest by any means, as the serpent beguiled Eve through his subtilty, so your minds should be corrupted from the simplicity that is in Christ [2 Cor. 11:3].**

I cannot overemphasize the need of more simplicity in getting out the Word of God. So many of our young preachers are the products of seminaries which are trying to train intellectuals. I was listening to one of these men the other day, and I couldn't tell what he was talking about. After about fifteen minutes, I was convinced that *he* didn't know what he was talking about. They try to be so intellectual that they end up saying nothing. What he needed to do was give out the Word of God. Oh, the simplicity that is in Christ Jesus!

Paul is still making an appeal to that minority group which had stirred up trouble against him and was trying to discredit his ministry. He has already explained the reason he didn't come to spend more time with them. He had not been called to be a pastor. He was an "evangelist"—literally a missionary who did not want to build on another man's foundation. He traveled onward and he moved out to the frontier. That was his service, his ministry.

Now he wants them to know that he is an *accredited* apostle. He writes, "I am jealous over you with godly jealousy." Why was Paul willing to actually make himself a fool, as it were, for them? Although he would rather speak to them about Christ than to spend the time defending himself, now it was necessary to defend himself—"So I am speaking foolishly."

He mentions this several times in this chapter. "Would to God ye could bear with me a little in my folly: and indeed bear with me," in verse 1. "I say again, Let no man think me a fool; if otherwise, yet as a fool receive me, that I amy boast myself a little," in verse 16. He says it is going to be necessary for him to defend himself, to speak foolishly. The Greek word which is translated "foolish" or "fool" can mean stupid or ignorant or egotistic. Literally it would be "mindlessness," with no purpose. Paul is saying that spending time in his defense is mindless because it is not getting out the gospel. It doesn't serve the purpose of his ministry, and yet he feels he must do it because of the opposition of this critical group in Corinth. This is why he asks them to bear with his folly, to suffer him to be foolish so that he can defend his apostleship.

We see the working of Satan in all this. At the very beginning of the early church the Devil used the method of persecution, but he found that he wasn't stopping the spread of Christianity. The fact of the matter is that the church has never grown as it did those first one hundred years after Christ lived. It swept across the Roman Empire, and by A.D. 315 it had gone into every nook and corner of the Roman Empire. That was during a period of persecution.

When the Devil saw that persecution would not stop the church, he changed to a different tactic. He joined the church. He began to hurt the church from the inside. He still does that today. He attacks the validity of the Word of God, and he tries to discredit the gospel. If that doesn't work, he tries to discredit the man who preaches the gospel. So he tried to discredit Paul.

Paul makes it very clear that he would rather be preaching the gospel than be spending time defending himself. He takes the time to defend himself because he is jealous over the Corinthians. He loves them. He is afraid they will be beguiled by Satan just as Eve was beguiled by his subtlety. Paul knows that Satan works "so your minds should be corrupted from the simplicity that is in Christ."

For if he that cometh preacheth another Jesus, whom we have not preached, or if ye receive another spirit, which ye have not received, or another gospel, which ye have not accepted, ye might well bear with him [2 Cor. 11:4].

We still face the problem today of the preaching of another Jesus, another spirit, another gospel. Some time ago there was a musical production called "Jesus Christ, Superstar," which denies His deity and presents a "Jesus" who never lived. It is the "Jesus" of liberalism dressed in a new wardrobe. And the Jesus of liberalism never existed. If they deny the virgin birth of Jesus, they are talking about some other Jesus, not the Jesus Christ of the Bible. If they do not believe that He performed miracles, they have a different Jesus in mind, because the Jesus in the Gospels is the One who performed miracles. He is the One who died for the sins of the world, which they deny. They deny that He was raised from the dead bodily. They deny that He is the God-Man. Yet one of the oldest creeds declares that He is very God of very God and very man of very man. If that is denied, then a different Jesus is being presented.

For I suppose I was not a whit behind the very chiefest apostles [2 Cor. 11:5].

I would rate Paul as the number one apostle; he says he is not the *least* of the apostles. He wants these Corinthians to know that he is just as much an apostle as any of the others. Just because he came to them as a tentmaker and because he walked in the meekness and gentleness of Christ does not mean that he is not an apostle. You see how Paul is forced to defend himself.

> **But though I be rude in speech, yet not in knowledge; but we have been throughly made manifest among you in all things [2 Cor. 11:6].**

Paul was a brilliant man, but he used simple language. There are two men who have had a great influence on my life. One was a scholarly man in Memphis, Tennessee, who taught in simplicity. The other was Dr. Harry A. Ironside who was known as a simple preacher. He was a brilliant man, but he preached with simplicity. He put the cookies on the lower shelf where the kiddies could get them. Simplicity was the method of Paul.

Paul says that he was rude in speech. I think that he actually adopted the language that the Corinthians would understand, and I am of the opinion that it may have been a rather rude approach. However, Paul was a brilliant man. From his writings I would judge that he had the highest I.Q. of any man who has walked this earth.

> **Have I committed an offence in abasing myself that ye might be exalted, because I have preached to you the gospel of God freely?**
>
> **I robbed other churches, taking wages of them, to do you service.**
>
> **And when I was present with you, and wanted, I was chargeable to no man: for that which was lacking to me the brethren which came from Macedonia supplied: and in all things I have kept myself from being burdensome unto you, and so will I keep myself [2 Cor. 11:7–9].**

Paul would not allow the Corinthians to contribute to his support at all. He had to work hard at making tents. Some others sent him some support to enable him to spend some time preaching the gospel, but the Corinthians did not help him. That his hands were calloused did not indicate that he was not an outstanding apostle.

> **As the truth of Christ is in me, no man shall stop me of this boasting in the regions of Achaia.**
>
> **Wherefore? because I love you not? God knoweth.**
>
> **But what I do, that I will do, that I may cut off occasion from them which desire occasion; that wherein they glory, they may be found even as we [2 Cor. 11:10–12].**

Paul says that he is boasting because it is the truth and because he is jealous over them and fearful for them. Other men, such as Apollos, may have been more eloquent and polished than Paul and did not stoop to do manual labor. Comparison with others is not the issue. Paul worked as a tentmaker. He did not take remuneration from the Corinthians. This does not detract from his apostleship.

> **For such are false apostles, deceitful workers, transforming themselves into the apostles of Christ.**
>
> **And no marvel; for Satan himself is transformed into an angel of light [2 Cor. 11:13–14].**

Evidently there were deceitful workers who attempted to make themselves apostles of Christ when they were not. They were actually servants of Satan.

People have the idea that Satan has cloven hooves and horns. This kind of erroneous idea comes from the great god Pan of Greek mythology, who was portrayed as half animal and was worshiped as Dionysus. Likening Satan to Pan certainly is not the scriptural point of view. Satan himself is an angel of *light*. If he would make himself visible to you, you would see a being of breathtaking beauty. Paul draws from that this conclusion:

Therefore it is no great thing if his ministers also be transformed as the ministers of righteousness; whose end shall be according to their works [2 Cor. 11:15].

The frightening statement here is that Satan has ministers. It makes your hair stand on end. As Satan is transformed into an angel of light, so his ministers are transformed as the ministers of righteousness. They are very attractive.

I remember as a boy in my teens I went to hear a lecturer from a certain cult. I was not brought up in a Christian family, and I didn't know how to differentiate truth from untruth. This man read questions from the audience. I am of the opinion that no one really asked this question but that he made it up himself so that he would be able to make a point. He said someone asked whether he could explain the halo of light that was around his head. Well, I took a good, hard look and I couldn't see any halo of light around his head. But don't you see what he was doing? He was making himself to be a minister of light. He was glorifying himself. All Satan's ministries glorify themselves. This is one way you can tell whether a man is preaching the simplicity of the Word of God or whether he is preaching some other Jesus and some other gospel.

I say again, Let no man think me a fool; if otherwise, yet as a fool receive me, that I may boast myself a little.

That which I speak, I speak it not after the Lord, but as it were foolishly, in this confidence of boasting [2 Cor. 11:16–17].

Paul says he must go on in this *mindlessness,* and they should indulge him in this.

Seeing that many glory after the flesh, I will glory also.

For ye suffer fools gladly, seeing ye yourselves are wise [2 Cor. 11:18–19].

He adds a bit of holy sarcasm.

> **For ye suffer, if a man bring you into bondage, if a man devour you, if a man take of you, if a man exalt himself, if a man smite you on the face [2 Cor. 11:20].**

He gives them strong reproof here. He says someone can come in to them, put them back under the bondage of the Law, he can live off them, exalt himself, smite them, and they will put up with that. They will take that kind of treatment from a false teacher.

Now we come to a section where Paul describes his own life as a minister of the gospel. I must confess that I have been in the ministry for many years but when I read what this man Paul went through, I recognize that I have just been playing at it. I have not been a real servant of Christ as this man had been.

> **I speak as concerning reproach, as though we had been weak. Howbeit whereinsoever any is bold, (I speak foolishly,) I am bold also.**
>
> **Are they Hebrews? so am I. Are they Israelites? so am I. Are they the seed of Abraham? so am I [2 Cor. 11:21–22].**

Paul says, "I can prove my genealogy." There was no question who he was.

> **Are they ministers of Christ? (I speak as a fool) I am more; in labours more abundant, in stripes above measure, in prisons more frequent, in deaths oft.**
>
> **Of the Jews five times received I forty stripes save one [2 Cor. 11:23–24].**

The Jews had a method in those days of delivering thirty-nine stripes, and to prevent killing the person, they would apply thirteen stripes on one side, thirteen stripes on the other side, and thirteen stripes on the back. Paul had had this kind of torture five times.

> Thrice was I beaten with rods, once was I stoned, thrice
> I suffered shipwreck, a night and a day I have been in
> the deep;
>
> In journeyings often, in perils of waters, in perils of rob-
> bers, in perils by mine own countrymen, in perils by the
> heathen, in perils in the city, in perils in the wilderness,
> in perils in the sea, in perils among false brethren;
>
> In weariness and painfulness, in watchings often, in
> hunger and thirst, in fastings often, in cold and naked-
> ness [2 Cor. 11:25–27].

How many of us today could say that we have been through even the smallest part of anything like that? We sit in the lap of luxury. We live in an affluent society. We know practically nothing of hardship for the sake of Jesus Christ.

> Beside those things that are without, that which cometh
> upon me daily, the care of all the churches [2 Cor.
> 11:28].

Those of us who are pastors have experienced the burden of a church. Paul had the burden of "all" the churches. We know a little of what that entailed.

> Who is weak, and I am not weak? who is offended, and I
> burn not?
>
> If I must needs glory, I will glory of the things which
> concern mine infirmities.
>
> The God and Father of our Lord Jesus Christ, which is
> blessed for evermore, knoweth that I lie not [2 Cor.
> 11:29–31].

Paul says, "Here is my report as a minister of Jesus Christ."

> **In Damascus the governor under Aretas the king kept the city of the Damascenes with a garrison, desirous to apprehend me:**
>
> **And through a window in a basket was I let down by the wall, and escaped his hands [2 Cor. 11:32–33].**

How embarrassing it must have been to have been let down in a basket! When I (and I'm sure other pastors have the same experience) go to a city to hold a meeting or a Bible conference, they always put me in a comfortable motel and are very hospitable to me. I am received with dignity. Imagine Paul having to be let down by the wall in a basket to escape those who were lying in wait to kill him. How embarrassing! Paul did all this for Jesus' sake.

My friend, don't brag about what you suffer for Christ. Read this over again. We must all bow our heads in shame and say, "Oh, Lord Jesus, help me to be true to You. Help me to be faithful to You."

CHAPTER 12

THEME: Revelation of Paul's apostleship

We hear a great deal in our day about space travel. This has been a big subject through the decades of the 60s and 70s. Men have been to the moon. Actually, that isn't really very far when one considers space travel. It is a long distance to the moon, and yet it is small compared to the distances to Mars and other planets. Then when one measures the distance to our neighboring constellation of Andromeda that is way out there in space, we must say that man hasn't been very far yet.

The very interesting thing is that the Bible has the record of three men who journeyed into outer space and then returned—none of whom are in the Old Testament. I know someone will say, "What about Enoch and Elijah?" I do not think they were caught up to heaven. The Lord Jesus said, "And no man hath ascended up to heaven, but he that came down from heaven, even the Son of man which is in heaven" (John 3:13). Some will say, "I thought Elijah was caught up to heaven." Yes, but after all there are three heavens. There is the first heaven where there are the birds of heaven. There is the second heaven where there are the stars of heaven. There is the third heaven which is the abode of God. Elijah had been caught up into the air spaces. Up to the time that the Lord Jesus made that statement, possibly there had been no one else who had been in outer space. He said that the Son of Man came down from heaven. Then we know of two other men who have been to heaven and returned. The apostle John on the Island of Patmos was caught up into heaven. He writes about what he saw and heard in the Book of the Revelation. He was in the third heaven where the throne of God is. "After this I looked, and, behold, a door was opened in heaven: and the first voice which I heard was as it were of a trumpet talking with me; which said, Come up hither, and I will shew thee things which must be hereafter. And immediately I was in the spirit; and, behold, a throne was set in heaven, and one sat on the throne" (Rev. 4:1–2). Paul was the other man who was taken up into heaven. The record of this is in the chapter before us.

Therefore there are three men who have been able to report from heaven. The Lord Jesus, who is God manifest in the flesh, said more about heaven than anyone else did, and yet He really said very little about it. John doesn't have too much to say about it. Paul doesn't have anything to say about it.

Paul tells us something here that he would not have mentioned at all if he had not been forced to defend his apostleship. He tells about his trip into outer space.

PAUL'S EXPERIENCE

It is not expedient for me doubtless to glory. I will come to visions and revelations of the Lord [2 Cor. 12:1].

Paul had just listed many incidents showing how he had suffered for Christ's sake. There wasn't much glory in that. I think that the Spirit of God had him write down all his experiences so that no man would ever be able to say, "I endured more than Paul the apostle."

Actually, we should be very careful about the songs we sing. I think of the one:

> "Jesus, I my cross have taken
> All to leave and follow Thee;
> Naked, poor, despised, forsaken,
> Thou from hence my all shall be."
> —Henry F. Lyte

I heard a so-called converted Hollywood star sing that song! I don't believe that person had given up very much. It would be hypocritical for most of us to sing it. It would be better if we all sang a song like this:

> "Alas, and did my Savior bleed
> And did my Sovereign die!

Would He devote that sacred head
For such a worm as I?"
—Isaac Watts

It is the Lord Jesus who needs to be glorified.

Today we hear testimonies from men and women about their conversions. Generally the testimony is a remarkable conversion. We don't often hear about the "ordinary" conversions. The thing which I note in a testimony is the place the Lord Jesus occupies. Too often the story goes on and on about the person and what he did and how he lived in sin and how remarkably he changed, while very little is said about the Lord Jesus. Sometimes one wonders whether the Lord Jesus was really needed or not. He gets very little praise and very little glory in most testimonies I hear.

I just received a letter from a man who said, "I turned from a religious system to Christ." Then Jesus became the center of his life and his sole occupation. He wants to grow in the knowledge of the Lord Jesus Christ. That is the thing that is important.

Having told us how much he had suffered for Christ's sake, now Paul will come to visions and revelations from the Lord. We already know that the Lord had appeared to Paul on the Damascus road. Have you ever noticed that Paul has very little to say about those personal appearances? Now here is another such incident.

I knew a man in Christ above fourteen years ago, (whether in the body, I cannot tell; or whether out of the body, I cannot tell: God knoweth;) such an one caught up to the third heaven [2 Cor. 12:2].

It was the Lord Jesus who spoke of the birds of heaven, which fly up in the air spaces. They don't go up very high. Out beyond that is the space that contains the stars of heaven. That still is not the same as the third heaven where the throne of God is to be found. How ridiculous it was for the cosmonauts in the Russian sputnik to say they didn't see God when they went to the moon. They didn't go far enough, friend. They must go to the third heaven to find the throne of God.

Paul speaks of his experience of being taken up into the third heaven. He dates it for us. He says it happened fourteen years before he wrote this epistle. That would be approximately the time when he had made his first missionary journey. We are told about his experience at Lystra on that first journey. "And there came thither certain Jews from Antioch and Iconium, who persuaded the people, and, having stoned Paul, drew him out of the city, supposing he had been dead. Howbeit, as the disciples stood round about him, he rose up, and came into the city: and the next day he departed with Barnabas to Derbe" (Acts 14:19–20)

Was he dead? I don't think they would have left him there unless they were pretty sure he was dead. It is my personal opinion that God raised him from the dead. Paul was rather uncertain whether this was a vision or whether he had been caught up in reality at that time. It is quite evident that he is describing his own experience here.

And I knew such a man, (whether in the body, or out of the body, I cannot tell: God knoweth;) [2 Cor. 12:3].

Was he actually dead and caught up into heaven? Or had he been knocked unconscious and had a vision? Paul is not dogmatic about it, and we should not be dogmatic about it either. As I have said, I believe he was dead and that God raised him from the dead, but the result was the same either way. He saw the third heaven.

Notice his report:

How that he was caught up into paradise, and heard unspeakable words, which it is not lawful for a man to utter [2 Cor. 12:4].

Most men would have written several volumes on ponderous tones on such an experience. And they would have given a whole series of messages about it. But this is all that Paul says. This is his report. He says so much and yet he says so little. There is no description, no Chamber of Commerce advertisement, no promotion, no sales talk, no display, no hero worship of man.

Of such an one will I glory: yet of myself I will not glory, but in mine infirmities.

For though I would desire to glory, I shall not be a fool; for I will say the truth: but now I forbear, lest any man should think of me above that which he seeth me to be, or that he heareth of me [2 Cor. 12:5–6].

There is no self-glory here. The man who was taken up into the third heaven and heard unspeakable words is the same man who was let over the wall in a basket.

PAUL'S THORN IN THE FLESH

And lest I should be exalted above measure through the abundance of the revelations, there was given to me a thorn in the flesh, the messenger of Satan to buffet me, lest I should be exalted above measure [2 Cor. 12:7].

Paul says he will tell us about his infirmities, but he will not tell us about the third heaven. Why? Because he was told not to talk about it.

I think many times Satan tries to remove God's witnesses from the earthly scene. He wants to get rid of them. He uses sickness, disease, a thorn in the flesh.

What was Paul's thorn in the flesh? I want to let you in on something, give you a little secret information which I hope you won't divulge to anyone: I don't know. I don't know what Paul saw and heard in the third heaven, and I don't know what was his thorn in the flesh. I don't know because he didn't tell us.

An old Scotch commentator said Paul's thorn in the flesh was his wife. Well, I'll imagine that old Scot was having trouble at home, and I think he was wrong. I believe that Paul had been married but was a widower. He wrote lovingly of womanhood, and I think he had once had a wonderful wife. He would not remarry because he didn't want to subject any woman to the hardships which he had to endure.

It is interesting that God put a zipper on the mouth of Paul and silenced him. He simply does not reveal these things to us.

Someone has said that the reason a dog has so many friends is because he wags his tail instead of his tongue! I suppose most of us would have wagged our tongues a great deal if we had been caught up into the third heaven. Now why did God give Paul a thorn in the flesh? It was to keep him humble, to keep him from exalting himself above measure, having had such a vision.

> **For this thing I besought the Lord thrice, that it might depart from me.**
>
> **And he said unto me, My grace is sufficient for thee: for my strength is made perfect in weakness. Most gladly therefore will I rather glory in my infirmities, that the power of Christ may rest upon me [2 Cor. 12:8–9].**

Now I have a notion that Paul's problem was very poor vision. When we get to his Epistle to the Galatians, we will find that he mentions that he had to write in large letters, which would indicate that he did not see well. We will discuss that later. Whatever the thorn was, Paul asked the Lord three times to remove it, and the Lord refused. The Lord heard him the first time and the second time and the third time. It was not that the Lord did not hear his prayers; it was that the answer of the Lord was no.

Sometimes you and I keep asking the Lord for something to which He has already answered no. If He doesn't give us what we ask for, we think He has not answered our prayer. More often than not His answer to my prayers is no. And eventually I discover that His no was the best possible answer He could have given me.

He said to Paul, "My grace is sufficient for thee." He said He would not remove the thorn but that He would give Paul the grace to bear the thorn. That is the wonderful thing about it all. "My strength is made perfect in weakness." In other words, it was obvious in Paul's ministry that he was so physically weak that the Spirit of God was empowering him. "Most gladly therefore will I rather glory in my infirmities, that the power of Christ may rest upon me." This was Paul's response to the Lord's answer. Paul would glory in his infirmities and not in the fact that he had had a vision. That is something you might turn over in your mind the next time you hear someone tell about a vision they have had of the Lord. It probably would be better if that person had a zipper on his mouth. The chances are that he had no vision at all but had eaten something he should not have eaten the night before.

> **Therefore I take pleasure in infirmities, in reproaches, in necessities, in persecutions, in distresses for Christ's sake: for when I am weak, then am I strong [2 Cor. 12:10].**

What a contrast this man is to Samson in the Old Testament. The Spirit of God came upon Samson and he became strong. People marveled at his physical strength, but there came a day when he was very weak. The strong are made weak, and the weak are made strong. God can use the weak man.

> **I am become a fool in glorying; ye have compelled me: for I ought to have been commended of you: for in nothing am I behind the very chiefest apostles, though I be nothing [2 Cor. 12:11].**

Notice how he elaborates on this. He is apologizing again even as he has done many times earlier. Paul considered himself the least of the apostles, yet he says, "In nothing am I behind the very chiefest apostles, though I be nothing." Someone should have defended him but, apparently, no one did.

> **Truly the signs of an apostle were wrought among you in all patience, in signs, and wonders, and mighty deeds [2 Cor. 12:12].**

There are certain sign gifts which were given to the apostles to authenticate their message. They had the gift of healing. They could raise the dead and speak in tongues, which does not mean *unknown* tongues but languages and dialects. Paul had gone through the Galatian country, and there must have been fifty dialects and languages in that area. Paul could speak them all. Had he studied them? No. In that early day it was necessary to get the Word of God out into the Roman Empire in a hurry, and so these apostles were equipped with these gifts. Today missionaries and translators must spend years learning the languages they will use. "Signs of an apostle were wrought among you." They could identify him as an apostle because he had the gifts of an apostle.

We have just come through a wonderful section of Scripture. Someone has said that one of the reasons Paul was not to tell us about heaven was because there would be a mass exodus up out of this world to get there. I don't know about that, but it is true that we could spend our time contemplating heaven and lose sight of a lost world that needs to hear of the Savior. Heaven is a wonderful place, but very little is said about it in the Word of God. Probably it is so wonderful that human language cannot describe it. It is our business to try to reach folk with the gospel so that they will be in heaven someday.

Although I cannot tell you much about heaven, I can tell you about the One who is in heaven. We can talk about Him, the Lord Jesus Christ, and we are to fix our eyes on Him. My, how this epistle has emphasized that! Beholding Him, we will become like Him in many ways. The pilgrim journey through this world will be a great deal easier if we will keep our eyes fixed on Him. The sun won't be so hot, the burden of the day won't be so heavy, the storms of life won't be so fierce if we keep our attention fixed upon the Lord Jesus Christ.

PAUL PLANS TO REVISIT CORINTH

For what is it wherein ye were inferior to other churches, except it be that I myself was not burdensome to you? forgive me this wrong.

Behold, the third time I am ready to come to you; and I will not be burdensome to you: for I seek not yours, but you: for the children ought not to lay up for the parents, but the parents for the children [2 Cor. 12:13–14].

Paul, you see, was their spiritual father. He had led them to Christ and had founded the church of Corinth.

> **And I will very gladly spend and be spent for you; though the more abundantly I love you, the less I be loved [2 Cor. 12:15].**

Paul says, "The more I love you, the less I am loved in return." It sounds like a complaint, doesn't it? But the Spirit of God insisted that he not tell about what he had seen in heaven but that he tell about his sufferings and disappointments down here.

> **But be it so, I did not burden you: nevertheless, being crafty, I caught you with guile [2 Cor. 12:16].**

Oh, notice this man. He says, "I wasn't after what you have, I was after *you*; I wanted to win *you* for Christ." Isn't that what the Lord Jesus had told His apostles? He said to them, "Follow me, and I will make you fishers of men" (Matt. 4:19)—and He didn't say that every fish they caught would have a gold piece in its mouth! He made them fishers of *men*—that is the emphasis.

> **Did I make a gain of you by any of them whom I sent unto you?**
>
> **I desired Titus, and with him I sent a brother. Did Titus make a gain of you? walked we not in the same spirit? walked we not in the same steps? [2 Cor. 12:17–18].**

Paul didn't use clever methods; he preached the Word of God in simplicity. He didn't send other men along after him to make a gain out of the Corinthians.

> **Again, think ye that we excuse ourselves unto you? we speak before God in Christ: but we do all things, dearly beloved, for your edifying.**

> For I fear, lest, when I come, I shall not find you such as
> I would, and that I shall be found unto you such as ye
> would not: lest there be debates, envyings, wraths,
> strifes, backbitings, whisperings, swellings, tumults
> [2 Cor. 12:19–20].

These are the things Paul expected to find in the church when he would get there. They expected a great deal of Paul. Paul expected a great deal of them. But what would he find? There would be debates and arguing.

I have been in the ministry for many years, and I am now to the place where I am in no mood for debate. Occasionally I get long letters from folk who listen to my radio program and want to debate a doctrine or a statement I've made on the radio. Friend, go on with your viewpoint and pray for me so that, if I am wrong, I will be led to the truth by the Spirit of God. You will not convince me with a long letter, because, frankly, I don't have the patience to read it. Someone may say that I am very bigoted and narrow-minded. Well, maybe I am, but I just don't believe that arguing and debating accomplish anything. Our business is to get out the Word of God, and I am not attempting to debate anything. I teach the Word as I come to it as I teach through the Bible.

The contemporary church is filled with the things Paul mentions here—debates, envyings, wraths, strifes, and backbitings.

"Have you heard about So-and-So?"

"No, I haven't heard."

"Well, I want to tell you."

Then they say some pretty mean things about a certain individual. And there are the whisperings. Someone has said that some people will believe anything if it is whispered to them.

Then there is that word *swellings*. I have often wondered what Paul meant. Probably the best explanation is the one I heard Dr. H. A. Ironside give. He said this reminded him of a frog sitting on the bank of a creek or a pond all swelled up. He looks twice as big as he would ordinarily be. Then what happens? You throw a rock at him and, believe me, he becomes little again and goes right down into the water.

Probably the best word that we have to describe "swellings" would be our word *pompous*. There are some pompous Christians.

"Tumults" are troubles in the church. Little cliques get together and they cause trouble. They circulate petitions to be signed and that sort of thing. That causes a tumult.

> **And lest, when I come again, my God will humble me among you, and that I shall bewail many which have sinned already, and have not repented of the unclean- ness and fornication and lasciviousness which they have committed [2 Cor. 12:21].**

Corinth was a vile city. It was known as a sin center throughout the Roman Empire. It was the Las Vegas and Reno and any other sinful city that you want to put with it all rolled into one. It was the place people went to sin. It is true that where sin abounded there grace did much more abound. Yet it caused the people of Corinth to look lightly upon these sinful things.

This does not present an attractive picture of the church, does it? I'm sure that as we have gone through this epistle you have thought, *The local church in Corinth certainly was not a very good church.* That is true. Not only was it true of that church, but it is also true of many of our churches today.

Let's stop to look at this for a moment. Suppose the Lord took the church out of the world right now. What would happen if He removed all true believers who are in the world? We believe that the Great Trib- ulation would then begin. A part of the contribution to the Great Tribulation will be the absence of the church. The church today is the salt of the earth, the light of the world, and the Holy Spirit indwells the church today.

Is the world getting better or worse? Some people say that the church hasn't improved the world because the world is worse now than it was nineteen hundred years ago. I disagree with that. I know it says in 2 Timothy 3:13, "But evil men and seducers shall wax worse and worse, deceiving, and being deceived," but that doesn't say the *world* is getting worse; it says that evil men will wax worse and worse.

I think this means they will get worse in their lifetime and then another generation will come on.

The world is a little better today than it was over nineteen hundred years ago because at that time the world committed a sin which would have been an unpardonable sin had not the Lord Jesus said, ". . . Father, forgive them; for they know not what they do . . ." (Luke 23:34). They crucified the Son of God. I recognize that the world today by its rejection of Jesus Christ is crucifying Him afresh. The greatest sin in all the world is the rejection of Christ. The world of each generation has been guilty of that. The Lord Jesus said that when the Holy Spirit would come, He would convict the world of sin, "Of sin, because they believe not on me" (John 16:9). There are many sins which are bad, but the worst sin of all is the rejection of Jesus Christ. The greatest crime that was ever committed on this earth was the murder of the Son of God over nineteen hundred years ago. The world today is still just as corrupt, just as vile, just as mean, and just as wicked as it was then.

I will say that the world today is a better place to have a home than it was nineteen hundred years ago. We can live more comfortably. There are a great many things which make life easier and better than it was nineteen hundred years ago. However, we need to understand very clearly that it was never the purpose of the church to plant flowers in the world any more than it was Israel's business to plant flowers in the wilderness. They were pilgrims passing through it and they had a message and a witness. This also has been the purpose of the church down through the ages.

The church is a group of people who ought to be holy unto God, ought to be living for God. I wish I could point to the church and say it is doing that and how wonderful it is. Its failure in this area is one of the reasons the present interest in the Word of God has in most instances bypassed the local church. It is too busy with its internal problems. Yet that does not destroy the fact that the church is that group which is loved by the Lord Jesus Christ. He gave Himself for it that He might wash it, that He might cleanse it, and that He might make each believer acceptable to God. Although we are far from what we should be, we should be moving in that direction.

So here in Paul's Corinthian epistles we have an insight into a church which was in the worst city of the Roman Empire, and how bad it was! I don't like to hear it said that the church does not in any way affect the world around it. It may look as if it has very little effect, and yet, then as now, if that group of godly people were to be removed from this world, the world would be much worse.

CHAPTER 13

THEME: The execution and conclusion of Paul's apostleship

EXECUTION OF PAUL'S APOSTLESHIP

**This is the third time I am coming to you. In the mouth
of two or three witnesses shall every word be established [2 Cor. 13:1].**

P aul is repeating what he has said earlier. He is going to Corinth for
the third time to exercise his office as an apostle. Everything is to
be authenticated when he gets there. Everything is going to be brought
right out in the open. Paul is going to exercise his office as an apostle,
and he is going to show proof of his apostleship by the power of Christ
working through Paul's weakness.

**I told you before, and foretell you, as if I were present,
the second time; and being absent now I write to them
which heretofore have sinned, and to all other, that, if I
come again, I will not spare:**

**Since ye seek a proof of Christ speaking in me, which to
you-ward is not weak, but is mighty in you [2 Cor.
13:2–3].**

Paul had come to them in weakness, but the Word of God was mighty
and had transformed them in that sin-sick city.

**For though he was crucified through weakness, yet he
liveth by the power of God. For we also are weak in him,
but we shall live with him by the power of God toward
you [2 Cor. 13:4].**

Paul says, "For though he was crucified through weakness." It sounds
strange to hear about the weakness of God. What is this weakness?

When He went to the Cross, my friend, that was the weakness of God. "Yet he liveth by the power of God."

Now Paul goes on to something that is very important. There is an inventory which every Christian should make regularly.

> **Examine yourselves, whether ye be in the faith; prove your own selves. Know ye not your own selves, how that Jesus Christ is in you, except ye be reprobates? [2 Cor. 13:5].**

This has nothing to do with free will or election or the security of the believer. Paul says we should examine ourselves to see whether we are in the faith or not. We should be willing to face up to this issue. I think two or three times a year we should do this.

When my daughter was just a little thing, she made a confession of her faith to her mother when they were back visiting her grandmother in Texas. She came in one day and said out of a clear sky that she wanted to accept Jesus as her Savior. My wife took her into the bedroom, she got down on her knees and accepted Christ. Regularly after that I would ask her about her relation to Christ. When she got into her teens, she asked, "Daddy, why do you keep asking me whether I am a Christian or not or whether I really trust in Jesus?" I told her, "I just want to make sure. After all, you are my offspring and I want to be sure." Now not only did I do that for her, I did it for myself also. I think every believer ought to do that.

> **But I trust that ye shall know that we are not reprobates [2 Cor. 13:6].**

Paul has made an inventory of himself, and he wants them to know that he is in the faith.

> **Now I pray to God that ye do no evil; not that we should appear approved, but that ye should do that which is honest, though we be as reprobates [2 Cor. 13:7].**

Paul is saying that he just wants them to be the type of believers they should be.

> **For we can do nothing against the truth, but for the truth [2 Cor. 13:8].**

Here is another great truth we should mark well. My friend, you can't do anything against the truth. That is why I don't worry about folk who are disagreeing about the Word of God. They cannot do anything against the truth. We should declare the Word of God and not spend our time defending it. God doesn't ask us to defend it. He asks us to declare it, to give it out.

> **For we are glad, when we are weak, and ye are strong: and this also we wish, even your perfection [2 Cor. 13:9].**

"Even your perfection" does not mean perfect as we usually think of perfection, but it means maturity. He wishes them to be mature Christians. He wants them to grow in grace and in the knowledge of Christ Jesus. We still hear that expression today—"Why don't you grow up?" That is what Paul is saying to them. Grow up in Christ!

> **Therefore I write these things being absent, lest being present I should use sharpness, according to the power which the Lord hath given me to edification, and not to destruction [2 Cor. 13:10].**

Paul is glad he can write to them at this time. He is writing for the purpose of building them up and not tearing them down.

CONCLUSION OF PAUL'S APOSTLESHIP

> **Finally, brethren, farewell. Be perfect, be of good comfort, be of one mind, live in peace; and the God of love and peace shall be with you [2 Cor. 13:11].**

Again he says, "Be perfect"—grow up. Stop being baby Christians. That is something which could be said to many believers today.

"Be of good comfort." He goes back to the word he used when he began this letter—the comfort of God. Remember that it means *help*. It means God is the One who is called to our side to help us, to strengthen us, to encourage us. God wants to do that for you today, my friend. No matter who you are, where you are, or how you are, God wants to help you. He can help you through His Word by means of the ministering of the Holy Spirit.

What great verses these are. God is with us to comfort us. We are to grow and mature. We can do nothing against the truth, but for the truth. Certainly we ought to go forward for God with such encouragement.

"Be of one mind" means to have the mind of Christ.

"Live in peace." We cannot make peace, but we can live in peace.

"And the God of love and peace shall be with you." This is the peace of God which passeth all understanding. It is the peace that God made through the blood of the Cross. We are to live in that peace today. We are to rejoice in our salvation.

The God of love and peace shall be "with you." Don't miss that. You are not alone—God is *with* you today. How wonderful that is.

Greet one another with an holy kiss [2 Cor. 13:12].

I hope you won't mind my telling you a story about the late Dr. Walter Wilson. A friend came to see him and his lovely wife. The friend greeted Dr. Wilson with a kiss because he was such a wonderful saint of God. Then he kissed his wife. He said to Dr. Wilson, "Now when I greet you, it is a holy kiss, but when I kiss your wife—wow!" May I say to you, my friend, if you are going to kiss, make sure it is a holy kiss. I would suggest that we confine our kissing to those of the same sex if we intend for it to be a *holy* kiss!

All the saints salute you.

The grace of the Lord Jesus Christ, and the love of God, and the communion of the Holy Ghost, be with you all. Amen [2 Cor. 13:13–14].

I have jokingly said that the apostle Paul was a Southerner because he used the expression "you all." You know that I am from the South and so you will forgive me if I, too, say, "you all."

When he says that the blessing of the Trinity should be with "you all," he includes us with the folk in the church in Corinth. We ought to revel in all that we have in Christ Jesus: the *grace* of the Lord Jesus Christ, and the *love* of God, and the *communion* of the Holy Ghost. How we ought to bear witness not only to the world but also to our own churches.

BIBLIOGRAPHY

(Recommended for Further Study)

Boyer, James L. *For a World Like Ours: Studies in I Corinthians*. Grand Rapids, Michigan: Baker Book House, 1971. (Excellent for individual or group study.)

DeHaan, M. R. *Studies in First Corinthians*. Grand Rapids, Michigan: Zondervan Publishing House, 1956.

Gromacki, Robert G. *Called to Be Saints* (I Corinthians). Grand Rapids, Michigan: Baker Book House, n.d.

Gromacki, Robert G. *Stand Firm in the Faith* (II Corinthians). Grand Rapids, Michigan: Baker Book House, 1978.

Hodge, Charles. *An Exposition of First and Second Corinthians*. Carlisle, Pennsylvania: The Banner of Truth Trust, 1869. (For advanced students.)

Hughes, Philip E. *Paul's Second Epistle to the Corinthians*. Grand Rapids, Michigan: Wm. B. Eerdmans Publishing Co., 1962. (A comprehensive study.)

Ironside, H. A. *Addresses on First Corinthians*. Neptune, New Jersey: Loizeaux Brothers, 1938. (A fine survey.)

Kelly, William. *Notes on the First Epistle to the Corinthians*. Addison, Illinois: Bible Truth Publishers, 1878.

Kelly, William. *Notes on the Second Epistle to the Corinthians*. Addison, Illinois: Bible Truth Publishers, 1882.

Kent, Homer A., Jr. *A Heart Opened Wide: Studies in II Corinthians*. Grand Rapids, Michigan: Baker Book House, 1982. (Excellent.)

Luck, G. Coleman. *First Corinthians*. Chicago, Illinois: Moody Press, 1958. (A good survey.)

Luck, G. Coleman. *Second Corinthians*. Chicago, Illinois: Moody Press, 1960. (A good survey.)

Morgan, G. Campbell. *The Corinthian Letters of Paul*. Westwood, New Jersey: Fleming H. Revell Co., 1946.

Morris, Leon. *The First Epistle to the Corinthians*. Grand Rapids, Michigan: Wm. B. Eerdmans Publishing Co., 1958.

Moule, Handley C. G. *The Epistle of Second Corinthians*. Fort Washington, Pennsylvania: Christian Literature Crusade, n.d.

Robertson, A. T. *The Glory of the Ministry*. Grand Rapids, Michigan: Baker Book House, 1911. (Deals with II Corinthians 2:12—6:10, and should be read by every Christian worker.)

Tasker, R. V. G. *The Second Epistle of Paul to the Corinthians*. Grand Rapids, Michigan: Wm. B. Eerdmans Publishing Co., 1958.

Vine, W. E. *First Corinthians*. Grand Rapids, Michigan: Zondervan Publishing House, 1951.